D6 Erweiterte Ausgabe

English G 21

Klassenarbeitstrainer
für Schülerinnen und Schüler

mit Lösungen
Lerntipps

W0394092

Deine **Audios** findest du hier:

1. Gehe auf scook.de.
2. Gib den unten stehenden Zugangscode in die Box ein.
3. Hab viel Spaß mit den Audios.

Dein Zugangscode auf
www.scook.de | opnhd-ph9t5

Cornelsen

English G 21 • Band D 6 Erweiterte Ausgabe

Klassenarbeitstrainer mit Lösungen und Lerntipps

Konzeption
Dr. Ursula Mulla und Nogi Mulla, Germering

Erarbeitet von
Bärbel Schweitzer M.A., Staufen

In Zusammenarbeit mit der Englischredaktion
Dr. Christiane Kallenbach (Projektleitung)
Ulrike Berendt (verantwortliche Redakteurin), Doreen Arnold
Susanne Bennetreu, Stefanie Juhnke (Bildredaktion)

Beratende Mitwirkung
Helge Kipp, Mülheim an der Ruhr
Martina Schroeder, Stedtlingen

Tonaufnahmen
Clarity Studio Berlin

Bildquellen
Alamy, Abingdon (S. 6: Catchlight Visual Services; S. 10 li.: Juice Images (RF); S. 14: HA Photos (RF); S. 20: Image Source (RF); S. 27: Erik Palmer (RF); S. 37: David J. Green; S. 38: UpperCut Images (RF); S. 54: Angela Hampton Picture Library); **Cinetext**, Frankfurt/Main (S. 22: Concorde); **Corbis**, Düsseldorf (S. 8: Ocean (RF); S. 47: Demotix/Demotix/Lois); **Getty Images**, München (S. 10 unten: Wolfgang Weinhäupl, S. 16: Peter Dazeley; S. 41: Daniel Schoenen); **Randy Glasbergen**, Sherburne (S. 42 oben u. unten); **iStockphoto**, Calgary (S. 7: Jasmin Awad; S. 9: apomares; S. 19: JohnnyGreig; S. 24 oben: VMJones; S. 33 oben: scanrail, unten: arattansi; S. 36 li.: laflor, re.: georgemuresan; S. 51 unten li.: drbimages, unten re.: hjalmeida); **Shutterstock**, New York (S. 4: Greg Epperson; S. 5 li.: spotmatik, 2. v. li.: Andresr, 2. v. re. oben: mangostock, 2. v. re. unten: Dmitriy Shironosov, re.: Olga Reutska; S:10 oben: Trevor kelly; S. 13: mangostock; S. 21 li.: Shutterstock.com/s_bukley, Mitte: Shutterstock.com/ Rena Schild, re.: Shutterstock.com/Featureflash; S. 24 unten: olly; S. 29: JustASC; S. 34 re.: ssuaphotos, Mitte: Yuri Arcurs, li.: Shutterstock.com/Stefan Glebowski; S. 35: MANDY GODBEHEAR; S. 43: Goodluz; S. 44: Vlue; S. 45 li.: juan carlos tinjaca, re.: Rui Vale de Sousa; S. 50: BigganVi; S. 51 re. oben: Elena Elisseeva, li. oben: Andrey Shadrin, li. Mitte: .shock; S. 53: servantes; S. 57: Pojoslaw; S. 60: Simone van den Berg; S. 62: YanLev)

Textquellen
S. 25: Abridged and adapted from "Teens would rather lose TV than internet or mobile survey" by Charles Arthur. Copyright Guardian News and Media Ltd 2012; S. 39: Abridged and adapted from: http://eusew.eu/. (Stand: 29.5.2012); S. 41: Abridged and adapted from "Hermann will den Radverkehr verdoppeln." © dpa; S. 54–55: Abridged and adapted from: http://www.london.gov.uk/young-london/teens/have-your-say/yl-survey.jsp#2. (Stand: 10.6.2012). With special thanks to the Greater London Authority for permission to cite from the publication of the Young Londoners Survey.

Titelbild
Getty Images, München: (woman (M): Erik Isakson (RF))

Layout und technische Umsetzung
Heike Freund, Hameln

Umschlaggestaltung
Klein & Halm Grafikdesign, Berlin

www.cornelsen.de
www.EnglishG.de

1. Auflage, 4. Druck 2020

Druck: H. Heenemann, Berlin

ISBN 978-3-06-032993-9

PEFC
PEFC/04-31-1156

PEFC zertifiziert
Dieses Produkt stammt aus nachhaltig bewirtschafteten Wäldern und kontrollierten Quellen.

www.pefc.de

INHALT

Klassenarbeiten, Vorbereitung auf die Prüfung, Prüfungen ...

... ist das 10. Schuljahr wirklich eine solch große Hürde?

Liebe Schülerin, lieber Schüler,

blickst du noch ein bisschen unsicher in das 10. Schuljahr? Denkst du mit gemischten Gefühlen an den Abschluss am Ende des Schuljahres?

Das ist ganz normal.

Das 10. Schuljahr ist ein gezieltes Hinarbeiten auf das Ende deiner Schullaufbahn. Mit intensiver Vorbereitung von Anfang an kannst du den Klassenarbeiten und dann auch der Prüfung gelassen entgegenblicken. Der Klassenarbeitstrainer unterstützt dich ganz gezielt bei der Vorbereitung auf die Klassenarbeiten.

Zu jeder Unit findest du zwei Klassenarbeiten, mit denen du alle Fertigkeiten (skills) trainieren kannst, die du für die Klassenarbeiten brauchst. In jeder Unit werden eine, manchmal sogar zwei Kompetenzen verstärkt geübt. In Unit 1 geht es gleich los mit dem Listening, in Unit 2 werden Reading und Mediation intensiver geübt und in Unit 3 ist das Writing mit zwei umfangreichen Aufgaben an der Reihe. In allen drei Units findest du zusätzliche Übungen zur Wiederholung wichtiger Grammatikkapitel. Du erkennst sie an dem Hinweis „REVISION +". Mit Abschluss der Unit 3 kannst du dann der Prüfung getrost entgegen blicken.

Wichtig ist, dass du dich den Herausforderungen der 10. Klasse stellst, indem du sie gezielt angehst und heute noch mit der Vorbereitung mit Hilfe des Klassenarbeitstrainers beginnst. Arbeite regelmäßig mit dem Klassenarbeitstrainer und überprüfe deine Ergebnisse sorgfältig mit dem Lösungsheft. Viele Aufgaben kannst du nach einiger Zeit auch ein zweites oder drittes Mal bearbeiten. Du hast dann die Möglichkeit, Probleme vom letzten Mal direkt anzugehen und dich so kontinuierlich zu verbessern.

Ich wünsche dir alles Gute und – auch wenn's manchmal mühsam ist – viel Freude beim Lernen.

Get started right away and be successful ...

Bärbel Schweitzer

Klassenarbeit A

Gesamtpunktzahl ______ / 115 Note ______

LISTENING

______ / 45

01 1 A radio phone-in – today's topic: How did you meet your partner?

______ / 26

a) *Read the task. Then listen to Lisa. Do the multiple choice tasks and tick the best answer to each question. (4P)*

1 Lisa talks about	a) her birthday and the day before.	
	b) her 20th birthday.	
	c) a man in her evening classes.	
	d) her birthday presents.	

2 The young man	a) used his credit card.	
	b) didn't want to have the money back.	
	c) was standing behind Lisa.	
	d) wanted to go to Lisa's party.	

3 Lisa and the young man	a) drank a bottle of French wine together.	
	b) started going out after her party.	
	c) want to get married soon.	
	d) want to have at least three children.	

4 After Lisa's story, the reporter says that	a) another person is going to tell their story.	
	b) there is a break now.	
	c) he liked the story.	
	d) they are going to play a love song.	

02 ***b)*** *Read the task. Then listen to Nick. Then answer the questions in a few words only. (6P)*

> **Notizen machen während des Hörens**
> Natürlich kannst du dir während des Hörens auch Notizen machen, um die Fragen im Nachhinein leichter beantworten zu können. Dazu musst du schnell schreiben können. Außerdem ist es gut, wenn du dir ein paar Abkürzungen überlegst, die du immer verwendest. Achte besonders auch auf Zahlen und schreibe sie mit.
> Finde selbst heraus, wie du die Aufgaben besser lösen kannst: mit oder ohne Notizen.

1 Where did the girl live before she came to Bristol?

____

2 What did the boys do to impress her? *(Give three examples)*

____

3 Where did Nick and the girl meet one day?

____

4 Why did they work together?

____

5 How long had they been together?

____

6 How can you tell that they're still friends?

____

03 ***c)*** *Listen to Anna. Then complete the sentences. (8P)*

1 Anna got to know her boyfriend ______________________________

______________________________. *(Give two facts)*

2 Her cousin is from Germany, and her husband ______________________________.

3 Anna sat next to ______________________________.

4 The German boy ______________________________.

5 Their conversation got better when they ______________________________.

6 On the day after the wedding party ______________________________.

7 When Anna has finished college, she ______________________________.

04 ***d)*** *Listen to Leo. Then say whether the sentences are* ***right*** *or* ***wrong****.*
Tick the correct box. (5P)

		right	wrong
1	Leo had invited a friend to a dancing club.		
2	There were more boys than girls.		
3	Leo talked a lot to the nice girl.		
4	Leo had some problems with dancing.		
5	Perhaps Leo will go to the classes again.		

e) *Correct the wrong statements. You may listen again. (3P)*

____

____

____

____

____

05 2 At the café

____ / 19

a) *Read the sentences below. Then listen to the dialogue and put the sentences in the correct order. (8P)*

	A	Jonathan has to go back to work.
	B	Jonathan is sitting at a table in a café.
	C	Catherine looks at adverts in the newspaper.
	D	Catherine gives some information about her future plans.
	E	Catherine comes into the café.
	F	Jonathan gives some information about himself.
	G	Catherine likes one of his ideas.
	H	Jonathan has some suggestions for Catherine.

b) *Listen to the dialogue again. Then complete the mind map. (11P)*

About Jonathan

About Catherine

Why Catherine needs a part-time job

Jonathan's suggestions for a part-time job

Catherine's jobs so far

LANGUAGE

___ /38

1 WORDS Me and my friends

___ /8

Complete the text with words from Unit 1. The letters in the blue boxes will give you another adjective for a friend who is good and reliable.

I have many friends, boys and girls. Their a _ _ _ _ _ _ _ _ _ is different. Most of them are quite t _ _ _, some have s _ _ _ _ _ _ _ hair, only three of them have c _ _ _ _ hair. Some of the girls are really g _ _ _-l _ _ _ _ _ _ and a _ _ _ _ _ _ _ _ _. I don't like a _ _ _ _ _ _ _ people, so of course all of them are really c _ _ _ _ _ _ _.

Ah, you want to know some things about me too? Well, I think I'm a l _ _ _ _ _ _ person with a good s _ _ _ _ _ _ h _ _ _ _ _. I don't like working so much so some people say that I'm l _ _ _. But I laugh a lot and I always talk to people _ _ _ f _ _ _ _ _ _ _ w _ _. And I should also m _ _ _ _ _ _ that I m _ _ _ f _ _ _ _ _ _ _ _ _ _ people easily and that I like to f _ _ _ _ with the girls.

2 GRAMMAR My friends and their hobbies

____ / 14

Lucy is talking about her friends. Complete the sentences with the ***simple present*** *or* ***present progressive****.*

Verwendung von simple present und present progressive
Das **simple present** wird verwendet, wenn eine Handlung regelmäßig, oft oder nie geschieht. Es wird auch verwendet, um über Dauerzustände zu sprechen.

Das **present progressive** wird meist bei Handlungen verwendet, die in diesem Augenblick geschehen. Man nutzt es auch für die Beschreibung von Tätigkeiten auf Fotos oder Bildern.

	positive	**negative**
Simple present	I go, she goes, they go	I don't go, he doesn't go, they don't go
Present progressive	I'm going, she's going, they're going	I'm not going, he isn't going, they aren't going

Mara, one of my friends, ____________________ (love) taking photos. She always ____________________ (carry) her camera around. She ____________________ (not take) any photos of people, she always ____________________ (take) photos of nature. Here you can see her. She ____________________ (take) a photo of a flower.

Susan ____________________ (love) languages. At the moment she ____________________ (learn) Dutch. She ____________________ (speak) English, Spanish and Italian. She ____________________ (not speak) Portuguese but she also ____________________ (want) to learn German.

Here you can see Philip, Chris and Ava. They ____________________ (not like) watching TV, in fact, one of them even ____________________ (hate) it. Sometimes they ____________________ (watch) a film at the cinema. In this photo they ____________________ (play) one of their many board games.

3 GRAMMAR REVISION + A social day for Mike and his friends

____/16

Every year in autumn there is a "Community Day" in Mike's town. Everybody is encouraged to help make the town look nicer. Mike and his friends wrote an article for the local newspaper describing why they took part and what they did.

Verwendung von simple past und past perfect
Das **simple past** wird verwendet, wenn etwas zu einem bestimmten Zeitpunkt in der Vergangenheit geschah und das Geschehen abgeschlossen und vorbei ist.

Das **past perfect** drückt aus, dass etwas vor etwas anderem in der Vergangenheit stattgefunden hatte.

	positive	negative
Simple past	I went, I cleaned	I didn't go, I didn't clean
Past perfect	I had gone, I had cleaned	I hadn't gone, I hadn't cleaned

a) *Complete the sentences with* ***simple past*** *forms. Be careful: there is one* ***passive*** *form. (12P)*

"We had decided to join the 'Community Day' long before the actual day. We simply ____________ (want) to do something for our town. And we ____________ (think) it would be fun working together. It ____________ (be) our job to clean places inside and outside town. We ____________ (start) at the station where we ____________ (not find) a lot of rubbish. We ____________ (be) more successful when we ____________ (go) to the small river near our town. We ____________ (find) many different things: a lot of rubbish like paper, plastic and glasses, of course, but also a mobile phone, a watch and an old school-bag. After we had taken away all the rubbish, we ____________ (try) to find the owner of the mobile phone. As we ____________ (not be) successful in finding him or her, we ____________ (take) it to the lost property office. In the evening we ____________ (invite) to an Italian restaurant by the mayor of our town."

b) *Read the text again and find the two past perfect forms and underline them. Write a sentence to explain when* ***past perfect*** *is used. Then write three sentences where you must use the* ***past perfect****. (4P)*

I use the past perfect when I want to show that ____________

____

1 ____________

2 ____________

3 ____________

MEDIATION

___ / 14

Ein Freund, ein guter Freund

Deine Familie hat Besuch von einer Familie aus Frankreich. Jean, der 12-jährige Sohn der Familie, interessiert sich sehr für Filme und besonders für's Filmemachen. Ihr findet diese Ankündigung im Internet. Du erklärst Jean auf Englisch, worum es in dieser Ausschreibung zum Wettbewerb geht.

Gib folgende Informationen auf Englisch weiter:

1 *Erkläre das Thema „Ein Freund, ein guter Freund". Gib dabei mindestens zwei Beispiele, was in dem Film vorkommen könnte. (vier Fakten)*
2 *Was kannst du einschicken, um an dem Wettbewerb teilzunehmen? (drei Fakten)*
3 *Erkläre die Teilnahmebedingungen. (drei Fakten)*
4 *Informiere über die Jury und die Preise. (vier Fakten)*

Home | Über das Festival | Geschichte | Wettbewerbe | Kontakt

Ein Freund, ein guter Freund

Ein guter Freund ist viel wert. Überlege, was du mit deinen Freunden machen kannst und in welchen Fällen sie zu dir halten. Kannst du dich auf sie verlassen? Bist du selbst ein „guter Freund"? Wann hat dir ein Freund schon mal so richtig aus der Patsche geholfen? In einer Situation, in der dir sonst keiner mehr geholfen hat? Weißt du, wie es ist, wenn man z. B. von Klassenkameraden gemieden oder gehänselt wird?

In unserem nächsten Filmwettbewerb geht es genau um dieses Thema. Wie jedes Jahr suchen wir junge Regisseure, die einen Kurzfilm drehen.

Thema ist also: Mein bester Freund.

Was bedeutet es für dich, für einen Freund ganz da zu sein? Vielleicht hast du schon mal einem Freund geholfen, der Probleme mit seinen Eltern hatte? Oder hat dir schon mal deine beste Freundin geholfen, als du große Schwierigkeiten in der Schule hattest? Du kannst uns zeigen, wie du für einen Freund da bist oder wie dein Freund für dich da ist. Vielleicht möchtest du auch eine Geschichte über ein Tier erzählen, das dir besonders am Herzen liegt. Erzähle einfach drauf los.

Du hast mehrere Möglichkeiten, an dem Wettbewerb teilzunehmen:

Du kannst einen kurzen Film drehen, du kannst uns den Entwurf für einen Kurzfilm oder auch für einen Zeichentrickfilm aufschreiben.

Dein Film kann lustig, traurig oder verrückt sein – je nachdem was zu deiner Idee passt. Das entscheidest du natürlich selbst.

Wir jedenfalls freuen uns auf deine Idee.

Sie sollte bis zum 1. Februar bei uns in Passau sein. Die genaue Adresse findest du unter Kontakt.

Ein paar wenige Bedingungen gibt es, die du beachten solltest: Dein Film darf höchstens 4 Minuten lang sein, und du selber darfst nicht älter als 14 Jahre sein. Die Idee für den Film muss von dir stammen.

Die Jury besteht aus Erwachsenen und Jugendlichen. Der Film, der den ersten Preis gewinnt, wird auf dem Nationalen Filmfestival im Oktober gezeigt. Der Gewinner des 2. Platzes erhält 150 Euro, der 3. erhält 100 Euro.

Also, mach dich gleich an die Arbeit. Wir sind gespannt auf deinen Film!!!

1

2

3

4

WRITING

____/ 16

How I got to know ...

The magazine "Young Friends" has asked its readers to write articles on how they got to know a special friend. Think of one of your friends and write an article of about 100 words. Use the ***simple past****.*

Write about
- *when you met him or her,*
- *where you met him or her,*
- *how you met him or her,*
- *why you became friends.*

Gesamtpunktzahl ohne Speaking _____ / 73 Note _____

Gesamtpunktzahl mit Speaking _____ / 86 Note _____

READING

_____ / 10

YFC – Young Film Competition

About us | The competition | How to enter | Tips | FAQs | Archive | Film academy

Do you like watching films?
Do you have some good ideas for a film?
Have you always wanted to make a film?
And – are you now looking for a chance to make your dream come true?

YES??? Then YFC is for you. We want to encourage young people from 12 to 22 to use their ideas to produce creative short films, short films for young Canadian people made by young Canadian people. That's why we organize a competition every year. Write and direct your film with our help.

We are not looking for finished films – no, we simply want to see your ideas. So show us an outline or a summary of your film idea or give us an idea of the first scenes of your film. It doesn't need to be perfect.

Your film ideas should be based on one of the following subjects:
- relationships,
- bullying,
- the environment.

It's our job to choose the ten best ideas. Our professional committee will check all the entries very carefully.

The ten film ideas will then be produced here in our film academy during four weekends in January and February. It's going to be a training process for you, our young film-makers. This process will include all the different aspects of film-making, for example directing the film, music, special effects. Don't be afraid, there will be professional film-makers to help you and to work together with you. There will also be students from our film academy who will be ready to give professional advice. Get as much or as little help as you like and need.

After the films have been made, there will be a film festival in June. The ten films will be shown to the public.

There will be discussions on the films and in the final celebration the ultimate winners will walk on the red carpet.

There will be awards for the three best films.

For more details about the festival events contact us at yfc@yfcfestival-film.com.

YFC asks for your entries not later than 10 October. If you need some more inspiration, look at the Archive of previous winners. Visit our 'How to …', FAQs and Tips pages to get help entering the competition, then click the upload links below to get started!

We're looking forward to your ideas. Come on, get started right away!

→

Three friends from Canada have heard about the film competition. They have many questions. Read their questions and then answer them with one to seven words or numbers.

1 At what age can we take part?

____

2 Is it an international competition?

____

3 Our film idea is on sports, is this possible?

____

4 When will the films be made?

____

5 Where can our parents and friends watch the films?

____

6 Will there be prizes?

____

7 What must we do to find out more about the film festival?

____

8 What is the final date for our application?

____

9 Where can we get ideas from?

____

10 Where do we get answers to all our questions?

____

____

____

LANGUAGE

____/50

1 WORDS About films

____/5

Complete the sentences with words and expressions from the box. Be careful: there are two more than you need. Make sure you use the correct form of the verbs.

award • (to) be based on • (to) bet • costume • dramatic • environment • in fact • reviewer • romantic • (to) be set in • special effects • (to) star

1 Timothy works as a ________________ and writes about films for a famous film magazine.

2 Sometimes films are different from the books that they ________________________.

3 Susan likes films with friendship and love, she likes ________________________ films.

4 People who are interested in history like films that ________________ previous centuries.

5 Even if you don't like the story of a film, you might like the ________________________ and the ________________ of the main actress.

6 The Oscar is the most famous film ________________.

7 I have just seen a great new film at the cinema. You should go and see it. I ________________ you will like it just as much I do.

8 Pete wants to see this new film that ____________________ Brad Pitt.

9 Next week we are going to the cinema together with our teacher. The film is called "Let's go Green". The topic is our ____________________.

2 WORDS Getting by in English

____/4

Sage, dass ...

1 ... du keinen Kaffee magst und stattdessen Tee möchtest.

____

2 ... du den Namen nicht verstanden hast.

____

3 ... Ann sehr arrogant ist, anders als ihr Bruder Adam, der sehr charmant ist.

____

4 ... Julie im sechsten Monat schwanger ist.

____

3 GRAMMAR A survey on young people

____/7

Lucy and Frank did a project about what young people do in their free time. They interviewed three friends and wrote the results in a calendar. Look at the calendar. Then answer the questions below in full sentences and give the correct information if necessary.

A = meet friends
B = do homework
C = help parents
D = learn German vocabulary
E = play computer games
F = do sports
G = watch TV/DVDs

Monday	Tuesday	Wednesday	Thursday	Friday	Saturday	Sunday
Linn → A, B Dave → B, E Joe → F, G	Linn → A, B Dave → B Joe → F, E	Linn → B, D Joe → F, E	Linn → A Dave → B	Joe → F	Linn → A Dave → C, E Joe → F, G	Linn → A Dave → A

1 Does Linn ever do her homework on Thursday and Friday?

____

2 What does Linn usually do at the weekend?

____

3 What does Dave do twice a week?

____

4 What does Joe often do?

____

5 What do Joe and Dave never do?

____

6 Does Dave help his parents on Friday?

____

7 What do Dave and Linn both always do on Monday?

____

4 GRAMMAR REVISION + What will be in the future?

____ / 10

*At the film festival there is an interview with the young film-maker Joanna. Fill in the missing forms of the **will-future**.*

Interviewer We now have the chance to talk to one of our young film-makers here ... So, Joanna, thank you for the exciting film about the two friends. Now, let's talk a bit about your future. What can you tell us about it?

Joanna Well, I hope I ______________ (have) the chance to make many more films in the future, so that I ______________ (be able to) learn more about film-making. I hope I ______________ (go) to a film academy in the near future.

Interviewer We ______________ (be) glad to see more of your films. I'm sure you ______________ (make) other exciting films and ______________ (be able to) go to the film acadamy. Are there any topics you are especially interested in and are there others you are not interested in, Joanna?

Joanna Well, I can definitely say I ______________ (not make) any detective stories because I'm not interested in crime stories. I suppose I ______________ (go on) making films about relationships, I think this is something people are always interested in.

Interviewer Many people ______________ (be) happy to hear about your plans for more films. I'm sure you ______________ (become) famous.

Joanna Thanks very much. I hope so too.

Interviewer Thank you and goodbye.

5 GRAMMAR REVISION + My ideas for the film

____ / 18

Stephen handed in a film idea for the film competition. Today he describes where he got the idea for the film from. Complete the sentences with the ***simple past*** *or* ***past perfect****. Be careful: there is one* ***passive*** *form.*

I ______________ (have) the idea for "Her Eyes" when I ______________ (be) in the swimming pool last summer. Suddenly I ______________ (see) this girl who ______________ (not be) particularly pretty, but her eyes ______________ (be) special. But I ______________ (not talk) to her. After I ______________ (leave) the swimming pool, I still ______________ (think) about her eyes and ______________ (start) making up a love story. First I ______________ (not write) down anything, I just ______________ (think) of ideas. But because I ______________ (not write) down my ideas, I soon ______________ (forget) them. So I ______________ (decide) to write them on small pieces of paper. That ______________ (be) a really good idea. After about three weeks I ______________ (collect) all my ideas and I then ______________ (write) down everything. The film ______________ (produce) this year in February.

6 GRAMMAR REVISION + A backstage meeting

_____ / 6

You have won a backstage meeting with a famous person. Choose a person you would like to meet. It can be a famous singer, an actor, a politician, ...
You want to write an interview for the "Young Page" of your local daily newspaper.
The day before you go to the meeting you work out your questions. Think of six or more questions.

☞ Hilfe für die Bildung von Fragen findest du im Grammar File 2 auf S. 161 in deinem Englischbuch.

MEDIATION

____/ 13

Almanya – Willkommen in Deutschland

You have an English friend who is interested in the film "Almanya – Willkommen in Deutschland". Explain in English what the film is about and give the most important details.

Der sechsjährige Cenk Yilmaz fragt sich, ob er Deutscher oder Türke ist. Seine 22-jährige Cousine Canan erzählt ihm die Geschichte seines Großvaters und der Familie. Hüseyin kam als türkischer Gastarbeiter in den 1960er Jahren nach Deutschland und holte die ganze Familie nach. Canan berichtet von den Anfängen und dem Leben der Familie in Deutschland, von den Träumen und den Schwierigkeiten im fremden Land.

Eines Abends überrascht Großvater Hüseyin seine Familie mit der Nachricht, dass er ein Haus im alten Heimatdorf in der Türkei gekauft hat, das als Ferienhaus dienen soll. Die ganze Familie macht sich auf den Weg in die Türkei. Es begegnen ihnen viele Erinnerungen. Schließlich nimmt die Reise eine unerwartete Wendung und am Ende bekommt Cenk eine ganz besondere Aufgabe.

SPEAKING

____/ 13

06 An interview with a young film-maker

Listen to the interview between Luke from the radio station "Younger" and Neil, a young British film-maker. He is 22 today, but produced his first film when he was only 17. Listen carefully to what Mike asks. You can take notes if you want.

____

____

____

____

____

____

____

Now you

Today you have the chance to interview somebody. Find yourself a partner. Look at the two posters and information about two films on page 24 that were produced for the "Young Film Competition" festival. Choose a film. You take the role of the interviewer. Make some small talk and keep the conversation going. Your partner can answer your questions with the information given on page 24.

Find out about
- *the content of the film,*
- *the idea for the film,*
- *the production of the film,*
- *the film stars,*
- *plans for the future.*

Here are some phrases that may help you:
- Oh, that's interesting. Can you tell more about this?
- So you have ...
- Another thing that I want to ask you ...
- Well, this is ...
- Now one last question, ...

→

Content of the film:
Shows relationship between an old lady and her dog, shows the normal day of an old lady, lives alone in a small house, only has a dog
Shows getting up, feeding the dog, going for walks with the dog, shopping in the supermarket, Mrs Creek only talks to the dog, dog is her life, her best friend, doesn't need a TV because of the dog, is happy

Idea:
From her own grandma who has a dog and doesn't talk to many people during the day but is very happy

Making the film:
Was rather difficult because of the dog, grandma liked it very much, she loved being the main actor in the film

The film stars:
Grandma Elly and her dog Romeo

Plans for the future:
Only 12, no real plans for the future, first it's school, school, school, loves animals very much, maybe wants to become a vet

Content of the film:
Funny, gives information about how to save the environment, Robinia (mother) cares for environment, for example: pays much attention to rubbish, different ways to save energy in the house, wants to make her family take care as much as she does (with funny actions)

Idea:
From a project at school (how to save energy, how to help the environment by small actions)

Making the film:
Directed the film and also acted, had clear ideas, professionals helped to realize them, added funny elements, had no idea about the music, but one of the film students added great sound tracks

The film stars:
Me (Samantha) as Robinia (mother), Rob (husband) and Cindy (daughter, 10 years old) (all of them friends of mine)

Plans for the future:
Most important: finish school, then film academy, later produce films, especially films about the environment

Gesamtpunktzahl ______ / 69 Note ______

READING

______ / 30

1 Teenagers and the media

______ / 19

The text about a survey on teenagers and their media is taken from the British newspaper "The Guardian".

New survey: Teenagers and their top three media

Young British teenagers would be less worried about doing without television than losing access[1] to the internet or their mobile phones, according to a new research.

Yet Britain's youngsters also watch more TV than at any time in the past five years, the survey found – though a growing amount comes through using online services such as the BBC's iPlayer. On average, they watch 17 hours 37 minutes per week, up from 15 hours 37 minutes in 2007.

Internet use has also become more popular, with 95% of 12- to 15-year-olds having internet access at home through a computer. But the research also points out that only 80% of children in lower social classes have access to the internet at home, compared to 98% in the richest ones.

A speaker of the survey said: "The almost universal use of the internet at home by 12 to 15s – both for their education as well as their entertainment – is a positive step forward."

The annual survey was carried out in spring with 1,717 in-home interviews, and focused on attitudes to communications technology by parents and children. It found that 28% of children aged 12 to 15 said they would most miss their mobile, and 25% would most miss the internet if it was taken off them – compared to only 18% who would miss television. A year ago mobile was the most desired with 31 %, while TV was on the same level with the internet at 24%.

Radio listening is also becoming less popular, with around half of those aged 12 to 15 not listening to any sort of radio, according to the survey results.

Parents are increasingly taking more care of their childrens' online usage, with the living room being the most common location for internet use, although a third of 12- to 15-year-olds have internet access in their bedrooms. The majority of those aged 5 to 11 use the internet with an adult in the room, but alone usage increases with age: half of those aged 12 to 15 used the internet alone. However, that figure has fallen since last year.

"The research also shows that parents and children are increasingly aware of how to be safe when using the internet," said one of the speakers. "But risks do remain. Better understanding – amongst parents as well as their children – is the key to helping people to manage content and communications, enabling them to enjoy the benefits of media use while protecting themselves from the potential risks."

Smartphone usage is also growing: around half of all children aged up to 15 have their own mobile phone, and the proportion with a smartphone is growing fast, having risen from 36% a year ago to 46% now. The use of mobile phones generally is also growing strongly among children aged 8 to 11, rising from 55% a year ago to 61% now.

Games console popularity seems to have hit a plateau, at between 81% and 92% depending on age, though the figures are almost unchanged from a year ago.

[1] access ['ækses] *Zugang*

Unbekannte Wörter erschließen
Um einen Text zu erfassen, brauchst du nicht jedes einzelne Wort zu verstehen. Es gibt aber unterschiedliche Möglichkeiten, ihre Bedeutung zu erschließen:

- In vielen Fällen ist es möglich, die Bedeutung unbekannter Wörter aus dem Zusammenhang zu erschließen, d.h. aus den Wörtern, die vor und nach dem zu erschließenden Wort stehen.
- Manche Wörter sind auch über die Kenntnis ähnlicher Wörter zu erschließen, z.B. kennst du das Wort „popular". „Popularity" ist das dazugehörige Substantiv und könnte im Textzusammenhang als Beliebtheit erschlossen werden. Allerdings musst du auf sogenannte „false friends" aufpassen. Das sind Wörter, die im Deutschen ähnlich aussehen wie im Englischen, aber trotzdem eine ganz andere Bedeutung haben, z.B. *I become, I will*.
- In vielen Fällen kannst du die Wörter auch über dir bekannte Wörter aus einer anderen Sprache erschließen, z.B. aus dem Französischen *historique, la politique*.
- Oft wird die Bedeutung von Schlüsselwörtern des Textes durch beigefügte Bilder klar.

a) *Read the text and find the missing information. Write short answers only. (14P)*

1	Name two things about teenagers and TV.			
2	Give the percentage of children from lower classes who don't have access to the internet at home.			
3	Name two things teenagers use the internet for.			
4	Write down the percentage of children who would miss their mobile, the internet and the TV this year and last year.		this year	last year
		mobile		
		internet		
		TV		
5	Write down the number of teenagers who listen to the radio.			
6	Name the place in the house where most children use the internet.			
7	Write down percentage increase in children with a smartphone from last year to this year.			

b) *Finish the sentences with information from the text. (5P)*

1 Not all children have ______________________________.

2 The annual survey was carried out ______________________________ this time.

3 More parents care about their children's use ______________________________.

4 Many of the younger children use the internet together ______________________________.

5 More than half of the children aged 8–11 ______________________________.

2 A do-it-yourself workshop

___/11

A do-it-yourself workshop

From our reporter Steve Collins in Brighton

Your bicycle is broken and you have no idea how to repair it? You need a new bicycle but have no money to buy a new one? You are looking for a special part for your bike? So read on and find out about a great new shop that has the answers to all these questions.

Emma's and Henry's bike workshop is just outside Brighton. There are many good reasons why people come to the shop. It's the place to go to repair your bike. You can use all the equipment and you don't have to pay much to do so. If you need a new part for your bicycle you will find a second-hand part in the workshop. The bike workshop opened only a few months ago but it has already become a hit.

Emma told me it was originally her idea. She had seen bike workshops in Vienna, London and San Diego. Back home in Brighton she knew she wanted a bike workshop here too. But would such an idea work in the small town of Brighton? Would there be enough people wanting to repair their bikes themselves? Emma knew that it was a big risk. But one day she rented an old garage and volunteers (that's what friends are for!) helped her to renovate as cheaply as possible. Today it's a comfortable place where people enjoy working. Meanwhile the do-it-yourself workshop has become more and more popular, and Emma needn't worry about paying the rent any longer.

When Emma got to know Henry, a car mechanic, she knew immediately that he was the ideal person for her workshop. Today Henry offers courses for everybody. "You have to know how a bike works before you can repair it properly," he says. "So I teach people some basics about bikes before we start repair them. Most of the people who have taken part in one of my basic repairing courses come back to our place whenever there is something wrong with their bike. They like the atmosphere here and of course the fact that we have all the necessary tools here. You don't need to buy a single tool, you will find everything in our workshop." And as I found out, this is absolutely true.

Emma showed me all the different old bike parts. It's amazing what you can find there. "Sometimes there are people who want to make their own bike, you know, they want to make an individual bike with old parts they find here. Or they take parts from their old bike and add new ones from here. It's a way of recycling bikes really. And it's a way of reducing rubbish." Fantastic!

The customers of the bike workshop are of all ages and of all professions. Some are students, some are nurses or shop assistants, some are university professors. Most of them can't repair their bikes at home because either they have no place or they don't have the correct tools to do so. What they have in common is their love of their bikes. So if you want to meet bike lovers, just go along and meet them there. And you will definitely meet me too!

→

a) *Read the text and tick the correct ending. (6P)*

1 Customers come to the bike workshop	a) when they are looking for a new bike.	
	b) when they have a problem with their bike.	
	c) when they are looking for somebody to repair their bike.	

2 Bike workshops	a) can also be found in other cities.	
	b) are always a big risk.	
	c) are run by people for their friends.	

3 Emma wasn't sure	a) if she really wanted a bike workshop.	
	b) if her friends would help to renovate the garage.	
	c) if she could earn enough money with the bike workshop.	

4 Henry	a) repairs the bikes.	
	b) thinks that people must get to know their bikes.	
	c) likes the atmosphere in the bike workshop.	

5 Emma is sure that	a) the bike workshop helps the environment.	
	b) everybody can make his or her individual bike with many different parts.	
	c) the author of the article will find the missing part he is looking for.	

6 Most of the customers	a) don't have much money.	
	b) would prefer to repair their bikes at home.	
	c) are a kind of bike fans.	

b) *You have read the article and decide to go to Brighton and meet Emma and Henry.*
Ask them ***five*** *questions about their work in the bike workshop. Use different questions forms. (5P)*

____

____

____

____

____

LANGUAGE

___/29

1 WORDS From the newspapers

___/5

Fill in the correct words from the box. Put them in the correct form if necessary. Be careful: there are two more than you need.

amount of • appliance • carbon footprint • climate • emission • fossil fuel • global warming • insulation • invention • power • scientist • target

1 Since 1970 British people need about 34% more energy. Use ______________ that save energy!

2 The latest figures show that UK ______________ fell by 7% in 2011.

3 Will Britain reach its ______________ and reduce its ______________?

4 Because of the warm winter, less ______________ was needed in Britain.

5 A Brighton high school student is proud of his new ______________. Look at his solar barbecue.

6 The ______________ of the town hall will cost more than expected.

7 ______________ is the most complicated environmental problem the world has to solve.

8 Greenhouse gases are mainly produced by burning ______________.

9 The ______________ carbon dioxide produced rose again.

2 WORDS A crossword

______ / 4

Complete the crossword with the missing words from the sentences.

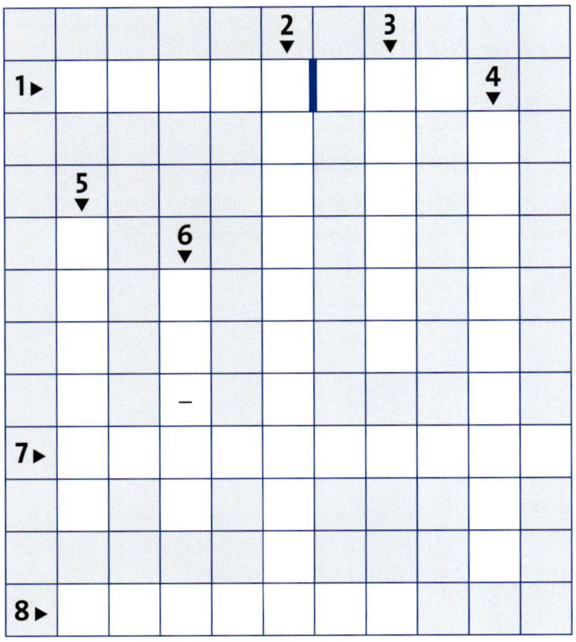

Across

1 I couldn't use the washing machine yesterday because there was a ... between 2 and 5 pm.

7 There are really good living ... around here.

8 I don't like people who only ... to care about the environment but don't do anything to save it.

Down

2 You are also ... for our environment and you have to try to save energy. It's not only "the others" who have to take care.

3 When you leave your house for holidays you should ... the coffee machine.

4 I looked at my friend's kitchen the other day. Believe me: there is an ... for almost everything in her kitchen.

5 My parents want to buy a new car. They have the ... between a normal one and an electric car.

6 Having the heating on while the window is open is a ... .

3 GRAMMAR REVISION + My bike is repaired

___/12

a) *Complete the sentences with the correct form of (to)* ***be able to****, (to)* ***be allowed to****, (to)* ***have to****.*
You can choose from the box. (7P)

> ☞ **can – may – must und ihre Ersatzverben**
> Wenn es um „können / dürfen müssen" in der Vergangenheit oder Zukunft geht, werden meist die Ersatzverben **(to) be able to – (to) be allowed to – (to) have to** verwendet.
> Wenn du dir unsicher bist, solltest du vor der Bearbeitung der Aufgabe im Grammar File 8 in deinem Englischbuch auf S. 169–170 nachlesen.

didn't have to • was able to (2x) • had to • was allowed to • wasn't able to • have to

Adam Have you got a new bike? Your old one is broken, isn't it?

Oliver I ______________________ afford a new one, so I repaired my old one.

Adam I don't believe it! Did you repair it yourself?

Oliver Yes, I did. I ______________________ do it with the help of the bike workshop down the road.

Adam Hey, it must be new. I haven't heard of it.

Oliver Yes, it is. It's great! I went there with my broken bike. A young man showed me round and then I ______________________ use all the tools they have.

Adam What about new parts?

Oliver Ah, good question.I ______________________ buy any new part. They supply hundreds of used parts, and you simply look for the part you need. Of course, you ______________________ pay for it. I also ______________________ pay for using the workshop at the end, but believe me, it was a fair price. I ______________________ pay it from my pocket-money.

b) *Think about going by bike, bus or car. Write* ***five*** *sentences using (to)* ***be able to****, (to)* ***be allowed to*** *and (to)* ***have to****. Use them in different tenses. (5P)*

____

____

____

____

____

4 GRAMMAR REVISION + About the environmental projects

____/8

a) *There have been many projects at Westland School during the last few months. Many of them have to do with the environment.*
Tick the correct ***relative pronoun*** *or* ***pronouns****. Also tick "not necessary" when you can leave the relative pronoun out. (5P)*

Relativpronomen
Relativsätze beziehen sich auf ein Nomen und bestimmen dieses näher.
Bei Personen verwendest du die Relativpronomen **who** oder **that**, bei Dingen **which** oder **that**.
Wenn das Relativpronomen Objekt des Relativsatzes ist, kann es auch weggelassen werden.
Wenn du noch unsicher bist, kannst du im Grammar File 10 auf S. 172 in deinem Englischbuch weitere Hilfen finden.

	who	which	that	not necessary
Mr Sunderland is the teacher ____________ asked us what project groups we would like to work in.	✔		✔	
1 The project were we plant trees is the project ____________ I like best.	☐	☐	☐	☐
2 Look, there is the girl ____________ is in the same project as me.	☐	☐	☐	☐
3 The head teacher is talking to the students of the project ____________ deals with the pollution of the air.	☐	☐	☐	☐
4 Sue and Carmelita are the two girls ____________ I work with in my project.	☐	☐	☐	☐
5 Alan is the one ____________ is responsible for painting the posters in his project.	☐	☐	☐	☐

b) *Write* ***three sentences*** *with two different relative pronouns. (3P)*

1 ____

____

2 ____

____

3 ____

____

WRITING

____/10

Gadgets on class trips

Read the following letter of an English head teacher to the parents and students of his school.
What do you think about banning mobile phones and MP3-players from school trips?
Is it OK or are there reasons why these gadgets should be allowed?
Write your opinion in about 120–150 words.

Dear students and parents,
Next week we are going on our class trip.
Therefore we would like to remind you of our school rules. Please make sure that the students do not take their mobile phones and MP3-players with them.
Many thanks.

Regards,
Andrew Johnson, head teacher

Klassenarbeit B

Gesamtpunktzahl ohne Speaking	_____ / 103	Note	_____
Gesamtpunktzahl mit Speaking	_____ / 123	Note	_____

LISTENING

_____ / 22

07 1 Talking about the environment

_____ / 8

a) *Listen to the text and complete the sentences. (4P)*

Bei diesem Hörtext musst du dich auf viele Zahlen einstellen.

One person in a car on a trip of 300 miles produces __________ kg CO_2.

One person on a plane on a trip of 300 miles produces __________ kg CO_2.

Four people in a car on a trip of 300 miles produce __________ kg CO_2.

Four people on a plane on a trip of 300 miles produce __________ kg CO_2.

b) *Complete the sentences with information from the text. (4P)*

1 Many people prefer flying because it's ______________________________ and it ______________________________

2 A longer trip by car can be cheaper than flying if ______________________________

3 If you use public transport, emissions are ______________________________

08 2 A family discussion

____ / 14

a) *Listen to the discussion. Then do the multiple choice task and tick the correct statements. (4P)*

1 Dad	a) tells his kids that he is going to sell the family car.	
	b) wants to make a difference and help the environment.	
	c) wants to get fit.	
	d) wants to go by bike.	

2 Sarah	a) sees a problem with the shopping.	
	b) is 17 years old.	
	c) wants to take a taxi to get home after a party.	
	d) wants to go on holiday by car.	

3 Sarah	a) doesn't like Chris's idea.	
	b) wants to have driving lessons with her father.	
	c) wants her father to give her a car as a birthday present.	
	d) worries that she cannot take all her suitcases with her when they go on holiday.	

4 Chris	a) likes his father's idea.	
	b) would like to use public transport.	
	c) wants to go on holidays by plane.	
	d) only has some information about another car sharing system.	

→

b) *Who says what? Read the following statements and decide if they are part of Dad's or Chris's idea for the car sharing system. Write the names after the statements.*
Be careful: one statement is correct for both systems. (10P)

Dad

Chris

1 In this system, you can register online.

2 In this system, you sell your own car.

3 In this system, people can rent your car.

4 In this system, you book a car on the internet.

5 In this system, you don't pay tax and insurance for the car.

6 In this system, you keep your own car.

7 In this system, you only pay when your car is rented by somebody.

8 In this system, the registration doesn't cost anything

9 In this system, you become a member of the organization.

10 In this system, you set your own rates.

LANGUAGE

____ / 40

1 WORDS The environment

____ / 6

a) *Collect at least six new words that have to do with the word field "environment". (3P)*

Climate, ____

____

b) *Choose three words from **a)** and write a sentence for each one. (3P)*

____

____

____

2 GRAMMAR REVISION + An old woman is talking about cars

____ / 18

*Complete the sentences with the correct verb form of the **simple present** or **simple past**.*

I can remember the times when nobody in our village ________________ (have) a car. And I still ________________ (remember) the day when the first car ________________ (drive) down the main street in our village. That ________________ (be) around the year 1938. Everybody ________________ (run) into the street when the car ________________ (come) nearer. It ________________ (be) an attraction for everybody.

Our family ________________ (not have) a car until 1955. My sister and I ________________ (be) very proud when our father ________________ (arrive) in front of our house with the new family car.

Today it's different. Almost every family ____________ (have) a car, some even ____________ (have) two. But things change: there are people who ________________ (not want) a car. They ________________ (use) public transport because it is cheaper and it ________________ (help) the environment. I ____________ (sell) my car ten years ago when I was 80. And I ____________ (give) my driving licence to the town hall on the same day. Today I ____________ (take) a taxi when I need to go somewhere.

3 GRAMMAR REVISION + A project for parents and young people

____/16

*Read the text and decide if you have to use the **active** or **passive**. Circle the correct form.*

There was an interesting project at Seaview High School last weekend.

The day **announced** / **was announced** on the internet as a hands-on day for children and their parents.

The police **wanted** / **were wanted** to inform the families about the dangers of the internet and how they can **protect** / **be protected** themselves.

A policeman **talked** / **was talked** about safety on the internet and **gave** / **was given** many examples of what can **do** / **be done**. Parents and children **ask** / **were asked** to tell the others about their experience with the internet.

A second important topic was social networking sites because they **use** / **are used** by more and more youngsters. Children **asked** / **were asked** what they do first when they come home after school. They **answered** / **were answered** that they **communicated** / **were communicated** on social networking sites for more than half an hour.

"The internet **gives** / **is given** you a lot of freedom but it also **takes** / **is taken** people's time," the policeman **said** / **was said**.

During the workshop the parents had to do several tasks. Many of them **helped** / **were helped** by their children. At the end, everybody **invited** / **was invited** to ask questions, and the policeman **answered** / **were answered** them patiently.

MEDIATION

____/24

1 An energy day

____/12

Ein Freund hat von EUSEW gehört und die Idee, einen solchen Energietag zu organisieren, fasziniert ihn. Beantworte seine Fragen auf Deutsch.

About us | Our Energy Goals | Energy Day | Projects

EUSEW – Organize your Energy Day

Every year hundreds of organizations and individuals in over 30 countries take part in EU Sustainable[1] Energy Week (EUSEW) by hosting Energy Day events and activities that promote energy efficiency and renewable energy sources.

Be a part of it this year by holding a sustainable energy-themed event, project or activity in Brussels or in your country between 18 and 22 June.

An energy day is a non-profit[2] making event, project, exhibition or display. It must take place between 18 and 22 June (weekends before or after are also acceptable).

To become an official EUSEW host, simply register your Energy Day. We expect to have more than 500 hosts across 30+ countries! Don't delay. Create a EUSEW account and register your Energy Day activity today.

Organize your Energy Day!

Be part of a European movement to promote energy efficiency and renewable energy by organizing an Energy Day. Get visibility for your organization, city or region and spread best practice. Get new members and read about your activity in the newspaper.

Submit your Energy Day! (You will be asked to create an account before you can register your Energy Day activity.)

Who are we?

The EU Sustainable Energy Week is an initiative of the European Commission in Brussels. Since 2006 hundreds of organizations and individuals have taken part in the EUSEW. They organize Energy Day events and activities that promote energy efficiency and renewable energy sources.

→

[1] sustainable [sə'steɪnəbl] *nachhaltig* [2] profit ['prɒfɪt] *Verdienst*

Tim Was steht da eigentlich über die EUSEW? *(3 Fakten)*

Du ______________________________

____

____

Tim Können wir das auch hier bei uns in Sachsen machen oder geht das nur in Brüssel?

Du ______________________________

Tim Ist das nun eine Woche oder ein Tag, den wir organisieren sollen?

Du ______________________________

Tim Und es muss genau in der Zeit vom 18.–22. Juni sein? Da haben wir doch unsere Parisfahrt.

Du ______________________________

Tim Also gut, ich stell mir vor, wir könnten da was mit unserem Fußballverein machen und uns nebenbei etwas für die Vereinskasse verdienen. Was meinst du?

Du ______________________________

Tim Was für einen Nutzen hätten wir dann für unseren Verein überhaupt? *(3 Fakten)*

Du ______________________________

____

____

Tim Das ist natürlich auch gut. Und was müssen wir tun, wenn wir mitmachen wollen? *(2 Fakten)*

Du ______________________________

____

2 Get on your bike

____/12

Your English penfriend visits you for a few days. He is very interested in environment protection and has seen this newspaper article. He asks you to explain its content to him in English.

Regierung in Baden-Württemberg will Radverkehr verdoppeln

Stuttgart. Die grün-rote Regierung in Baden-Württemberg will den Radverkehr fördern. „Unser Ziel ist es, den Radverkehr in Städten und Gemeinden innerhalb von zehn Jahren zu verdoppeln", sagt ein Sprecher der Regierung.

Kernpunkt der Initiative „RadKultur" ist, für stärkere Akzeptanz des Fahrradfahrens zu sorgen. Ein Expertenteam wird in den nächsten Monaten Vorschläge machen, wie das Radwegnetz ausgebaut werden kann.

Die Initiative „Radkultur" wird fürs Erste in Tübingen, Lörrach und Mannheim umgesetzt. Man denkt an Ideenwettbewerbe, will mit gezielten Aktionen an Schulen für das Rad werben und will Unternehmen als Partner gewinnen, denn auch Firmen müssen lernen, das Fahrrad als Verkehrsmittel zu akzeptieren.

Die Regierung stellt in den nächsten Jahren mehrere Millionen Euro zur Verfügung, um den Radverkehr im Alltag zu fördern.

Explain
- the government's target for the next years (2P)
- the initiative „RadKultur" (4P)
- where and how the initiative will be realised (4P)
- why companies take part in the initiative (2P)

New words
Expertenteam *team of experts;* akzeptieren *(to) accept*

WRITING

____ / 17

A car of your own?

Many young people at the age of 20–25 don't want a car of their own.
What's your opinion? Would you like a car of your own once you have a driving licence?
Write a text of about 160–200 words.

Think about
- *costs*
- *your carbon footprint*
- *time*
- *...*

Einen Text strukturieren
Dein Text sollte in drei Hauptabschnitte eingeteilt sein:
- in eine Einleitung, die in das Thema einführt,
- in einen Hauptteil, in dem du deine Argumente zu den einzelnen Punkten vorbringst,
- in einen Schluss, in dem du deine eigene Meinung schreibst.

SPEAKING

____/20

09 How ecology-minded are we?

Look at the cartoon and try to understand its message. Then listen to the CD.

"Explain to me again why our ecology textbook is printed on dead trees."

Now you

Look at the cartoon and try to understand its message. Then talk about the cartoon.

Divide your talk into four parts:
- *first describe the cartoon,*
- *say what the cartoon is about and talk about the message,*
- *give your opinion about the message.*
- *Finally, talk about yourself and your family. What do you do to keep your carbon footprint low?*

"We have a new line of environmentally-friendly shoes. They leave a low-carbon footprint."

Klassenarbeit A

Gesamtpunktzahl ______ / 109	Note ______

LISTENING

______ / 26

Great success for students

a) *Read the table below. Then listen to the radio show and complete the table. (14P)*

1 Name the months when timetables change.	
2 Give information about the experience with the timetable changes so far. *(2 facts)*	
3 Say when the listeners found out that the bus company had reacted to the protests?	
4 Give reasons why the bus company reacted.	
5 Give two facts about where Steve lives.	
6 Name three reasons why the new timetable was bad for Steve.	
7 Name three ways the new timetable affected Melissa.	
8 Explain why Melissa thought that the bus company's timetable changes were not OK.	

11 ***b)** Listen to the second part of the radio show. Then answer the questions. You don't need to write complete sentences. You can listen twice. (12P)*

1 How does the school teach the students democratic rules?

____

2 What activities did they decide on in class? *(three facts)*

____

____

____

3 What were the reactions to the students' activities? *(three facts)*

____

____

____

4 Why was the protest a good experience for the students?

____

5 What has impressed Mrs Miller? *(four facts)*

____

____

____

____

LANGUAGE

___/57

1 WORDS The wrong word

___/3

One of the four words in each group does not fit. Cross out the wrong word.

1 town hall • mayor • town councillor • political party

2 to have your say • to make sth up • to vote • to speak out

3 campaign • demonstration • trade • petition

4 to fight • to take action • to demonstrate • to make sense

5 novel • play • narrator • poem

6 democracy • prime minister • politician • member of parliament

2 WORDS Creating new words

___/10

Find words from the same word family. The words can be ***adjectives***, ***verbs*** *or* ***nouns***.

independent	independence
1 sense	
2 poor	
3 (to) think	
4 (to) annoy	
5 (to) debate	
6 (to) apologize	
7 (to) own	
8 (to) speak	
9 (to) feel	
10 discrimination	

3 GRAMMAR REVISION + A discussion about bus times

_____/9

*Before, during and after the students' campaign against the new bus times there were/are a lot of discussions. Here are some of the statements. Complete the **if-clauses** with the correct form of the verb in brackets.*

if-clauses – kurze Wiederholung

1	If	we	**go**	to London,	we	**will visit**	Madame Tussauds.
2	If	she	**had**	more time,	she	**would go**	to Paris.
3	If	I	**had invited**	her,	we	**could/would have talked**	to her.

Before the campaign

1 I _______________ (have to) catch the early bus at 7.10 if I want to be at school on time.

2 If the bus company _______________ (not change) the times, we will go on strike.

3 I _______________ (not be able to) take part in the dancing lessons any more if I don't get home until 5.20 pm.

During the campaign

1 If we _______________ (talk) to the bus company, perhaps they would change the times again.

2 We could tell a lot of people in town if we _______________ (go) to the market square on Saturday morning.

3 If we _______________ (collect) a lot of signatures from people in town, we could give them to the bus company.

After the campaign

1 If the students hadn't done anything about the new bus times, some of them _______________ (not have) time for hobbies after school.

2 If the students _______________ (not write) the letter to the newspaper, the public wouldn't have known about the issue.

3 If the students hadn't done such a good job, the bus company _______________ (not react).

4 GRAMMAR Teens speak out

____ / 10

Complete the newspaper article by choosing the right expression for the numbered gaps. Tick the answers in the table below.

Students had the chance to discuss problem issues

"Teens Speak Out" – 1 – last Saturday morning with a short speech and an explanation of Rule No. 1: "You adults out there – 2 – to speak now," presenter Phil Cross told the audience.

During the discussion, students shared their opinions – 3 – many different topics. They – 4 – about communication with teachers and the head teacher, the importance of sports and about school safety.

14-year-old student Alan said that it was necessary to improve contact with the head teacher. "The only time you hear from the head teacher is – 5 – an assembly, or when she's addressing all the students, or when there's something going on that she – 6 –," he said.

Sue, aged 15, agreed. She wanted the head teacher to see and recognize the good work that – 7 – by many students. "It's time the head teacher changed something. At the moment she only speaks to us when something is going wrong. Things would be much better if she – 8 – the good work and talked – 9 – the students about their – 10 –."

1	begins	☐	began	☐	begin	☐	has begun	☐
2	cannot	☐	allow	☐	aren't allowed	☐	has	☐
3	with	☐	to	☐	over	☐	about	☐
4	speaks	☐	spoke	☐	had spoken	☐	will speak	☐
5	during	☐	while	☐	on	☐	with	☐
6	don't like	☐	will like	☐	like	☐	doesn't like	☐
7	do	☐	is done	☐	did	☐	has done	☐
8	would see	☐	saw	☐	sees	☐	doesn't see	☐
9	to	☐	at	☐	about	☐	on	☐
10	succeed	☐	successful	☐	success	☐	succeeded	☐

5 GRAMMAR REVISION + Word order

_____ /8

Here are some notes from a students' meeting. Put the words in the correct order and write them down.

Die Wortstellung im englischen Satz
Bevor du mit dieser Übung beginnst, solltest du dir die wichtigsten Punkte zur Satzstellung im englischen Satz ins Gedächtnis rufen, z. B. S - V - O. Wenn du noch unsicher bist, kannst du auch im Grammar File 1 auf S. 160 in deinem Englischbuch nachlesen.

Report of March 13

1 great meeting / had / last week / we / a /.

2 for the School Yearbook / first of all, / a picture / took / we /.

3 the school shop / was / long discussion / then / a / about / there /.

4 enjoy / all the students / things / nearly / buying / at the shop /.

5 heard / we / what / like / needs / they / to be improved / and / what /.

6 the youth club / after that / talked / we / about /.

7 to finish / didn't have / unfortunately, / the discussion / time / we /.

8 we / next Saturday / so / meet again / going to / are /.

1 ______________________________

2 ______________________________

3 ______________________________

4 ______________________________

5 ______________________________

6 ______________________________

7 ______________________________

8 ______________________________

6 Everyday English: Solving conflicts

____ / 17

You are staying at a youth hostel in Sweden for a week. Ten people use the same kitchen, so everybody needs to tidy up after cooking and eating their meal.

A girl, Anna, has left the kitchen in a complete mess for the third time. As you want to use the kitchen now, you decide to talk to her. Make up a dialogue.

You	▶ start the conversation	Excuse me, Anna, can I have a word with you?
You	▶ name the problem	
Anna	▶ disagree that there is a problem and start talking about how wonderful your dinner was	
You	▶ explain the problem again	
Anna	▶ apologize, find a way to solve the problem	
You	▶ end the conflict and make a suggestion	
Anna	▶ say thank you and say that you like the idea	

WRITING

____/26

1 Young people and their attitude towards the internet

____/15

Young people who are very involved in different projects in their free time, have been asked about using the internet. First read the young people's statements.

The internet is definitely not safe. I'm worried that personal information might be misused.

Surfing the internet a lot means you don't have enough time to get involved in useful projects, e.g. volunteering to help others.

The internet costs a lot of money, and you can't concentrate any longer on things that really matter.

Using the internet is too expensive.

The internet is only for relaxing.

→

You have been asked to write an article for your school homepage.
You have to think about the question: "Do young people need the internet?"

Write an article of about 170 words.
- *Start with an introduction explaining the young people's statements about the internet.*
- *Give some information about the statements. You need not write about all of them.*
- *Give your opinion:*
  - *What do you use the internet for and how often?*
  - *Do you agree with any of the statements? Why/Why not?*
  - *What do you personally think about the internet?*
- *At the end, sum up your arguments.*

Wichtige Punkte beim Writing:
- Beachte die Aufgabenstellung genau, du kannst wichtige Hinweise auch unterstreichen.
- Vor dem Schreiben: Sammle Ideen (z. B. mit einer Mindmap).
- Strukturiere den Text (Einleitung, Hauptteil und Schluss).
- Verwende **linking words** (**time phrases**, Konjunktionen, Relativpronomen).
- Beachte die Rechtschreibung und Grammatik (richtige Wortstellung, Zeiten).
- Achte auf eine sinnvolle Länge der Sätze.

2 What about an environmental group at your school?

___/11

Your friend Steve is an active member of an environmental group at his school in the UK. In his latest email to you he asked you to start an environmental group at your school too. He thinks every school should have one.

Read his email.

Hi!

How are you? I'm working hard for my environmental group at school at the moment. We meet once a week together with a teacher who is very involved in the topic too.

Our results are good. There was an article about our group in the newspaper last week. They said that there should be an environmental group at every school. I completely agree!

Do you have such a group in Germany too?

Or can you imagine starting an environmental group at your school? What do you think about that?

What sort of activities would be best for your school?

Do you have any questions about environmental groups?

Feel free to ask me!

Write soon. I'm looking forward to your answers.

Yours,

Steve

What do you think about Steve's idea? Write an answer to his email. Answer Steve's questions in your email. Give reasons for your answers and say if you can or can't imagine starting an environmental group at your school.

Write about 130 words in your exercise book.

Klassenarbeit B

Gesamtpunktzahl ohne Speaking ______ / 59	Note ______
Gesamtpunktzahl mit Speaking ______ / 80	Note ______

READING

______ / 11

Report on young Londoners

Nicolas has found a report on young Londoners on the internet.

a) *Read the information about the report and then answer the questions in 1–7 words or numbers. (4P)*

In spring 2009, the Greater London Authority[1] organized a survey to find out more about young Londoners. The report covers young people's views on key topics such as education, crime and safety, getting involved in London, transport and the environment, and their attitudes to the main activities organized by the Mayor of London.
The results paint quite a positive picture of young people's lives in London, but also highlighted a number of significant problems which have to be solved.
More than one thousand young Londoners aged 11–16 took part in interviews between March and April 2009.
The survey was done to help us understand where we, the Greater London Authority together with the Mayor of London, can best offer our support to young people.
We also want to compare the results to the ones from the 2004 survey. And we want to use the results again in the future to find out what has been improved.

Abridged and adapted from: http://www.london.gov.uk/young-london/teens/have-your-say/yl-survey.jsp#2

1 What were four of the topics of the survey?	
2 Who was interviewed *(2 facts)*?	
3 Why did they need the 2004 survey?	

[1] Greater London Authority *Gesamtverwaltung für Groß-London*

b) *Nicolas has taken some notes about the report. Read the notes and tick the correct statements. (7P)*

Active and involved

Young Londoners are getting involved:
55% have taken part in at least one activity to support a change in their area.
More should be done to activate young people:
51% of those that haven't taken part say it's because no one has asked them.
Only 7% that haven't taken part say it's because it wouldn't make a difference.

Feeling safe

83% of young Londoners feel safe in their neighbourhood – up from 77% in 2004.
Young Londoners' biggest worries are violent crime, and their own safety:
27% feel unsafe because of knife crime.
22% feel unsafe because of possible attacks in the street.
22% feel unsafe because of teenagers hanging round.

Crime and feeling safer

A minority, but significant number, report having been victim to violent crime:
1% (or 5,000) report being a victim of knife crime.
5% (or 25,000) report being a victim of attacks in the streets.
39% of young Londoners said 'more police' would make them feel safer – the top answer. This fits with young Londoners saying that 'safety and not enough police' is the 'worst thing' about London.

Education, skills & jobs

Young people feel more positive about the quality of their schools.
94% say their school is good or very good.
London has opportunities, even in difficult times.
70% of young Londoners are confident, even now, that London can give them the job opportunities they want.

Taking part in decisions

In general young Londoners feel they can do something about decisions in their schools, but not in their neighbourhoods or London.
67% feel they can do something about school decisions (10% more than in 2004).
31% feel they can do something about neighbourhood decisions.
16% feel they can do something about London's decisions.

London's environment

Young people think environmental issues are less of a problem now than they were in 2004, but the problem still exists.
Around 8 out of 10 saw climate change, traffic pollution and rubbish as a problem.
Around 7 out of 10 saw pollution of rivers, air pollution and death of plants and animals as a problem.
Saving parks and green spaces is the No 1 priority for improving London's environment: 32%.
Waste and air quality were also important issues.

Getting around

Buses are young Londoners' main form of public transport:
64% use them every day, or every other day.
The Zip Card (which gives free bus fares to under-16s, and some under-18s) does not keep young Londoners from walking to school:
38% often walk to school – the same number as in 2004.

London as a place to live

Young Londoners are happy with where they live – 85% think their neighbourhood is OK, 84% are happy with London as a whole.
Young people enjoy many different people
37% named the 'mix of people that live here' as the 'best thing' about London, second only to the 'many different shops'.

1 When talking about living in London, shopping	a) is the most important thing for young Londoners.	☐
	b) only comes second.	☐
	c) is not mentioned.	☐

2 The 2009 survey shows that	a) most young Londoners have tried to change something in their area.	☐
	b) it's necessary to activate more young people.	☐
	c) many young people think you can't change anything by getting involved.	☐

3 If you compare the results of 2004 and 2009,	a) in 2004, fewer young people said that they could take part in decisions at schools.	☐
	b) more people felt safe in 2004.	☐
	c) issues about the environment were not a problem in 2009.	☐

4 When talking about safety and crime,	a) many young people say that they have been victim to violent crime.	☐
	b) teenagers hanging around is one of the biggest problems.	☐
	c) many young Londoners would like the police to be more present in London.	☐

5 The survey says that	a) most young people walk to school although they could use the bus for free.	☐
	b) young Londoners don't walk because of the Zip Card.	☐
	c) the bus is the favourite form of transport.	☐

6 When talking about the environment,	a) young Londoners make it clear that parks are very important.	☐
	b) waste and air quality are the most important issues.	☐
	c) more young people mentioned the pollution of the waterways as a problem than rubbish.	☐

7 Many young people think	a) that the quality of their schools could be better.	☐
	b) that they will find a job in the London area.	☐
	c) that London cannot provide good opportunities in difficult times.	☐

LANGUAGE

____/37

1 WORDS Have your say – a discussion

____/5

Complete the text with the correct words from the box. Make sure you use the correct form. Be careful: there are three more than you need.

annoying • campaign • issue • (to) make sense • mosquito device (4x) • petition • politician • public • (to) speak out • unless

Next week: Have your say – a discussion

The ____________ can take part in another discussion on an important topic on Wednesday, 7 July at 7.30 pm.

This time the discussion then will be on the ____________ which has been installed in front of the youth club.

As usual, interesting guests will take part and discuss the topic, for example Mr Pit Hank, a ____________ here in our town. Mr Hank thinks the ____________ is a useful thing and that it ____________ where it is. Then there are Tom and Nicholas, two students who have started a ____________ against the ____________. And there is Mrs Felder. Although Mrs Felder lives near the youth club, she supports the ____________ against the ____________. Also there will be Mr Jeff Saltman who says that the mosquito device can't be removed ____________ the young people get a new place to meet.

Peter Smith, the well-known presenter from Radio Young, will lead the discussion.

Place: Grattan's Hotel, 24 Swansea Road.

2 WORDS Students talking in a school break

____ / 6

Circle the correct preposition.

1 I think Jo is very good **at** / **in** presenting topics.

2 I'm afraid **of** / **for** failing our Maths test tomorrow.

3 Mrs Sutter is a really good teacher. Her attitude **towards** / **with** the students is excellent.

4 I can't blame anybody else **to** / **for** my bad mark in English – I have just been too lazy the last few months.

5 I'm glad that Sue apologized **with** / **to** me **at** / **for** her bad behaviour.

6 I read in the school magazine that the number of hours spent **on** / **for** homework at our school has risen **at** / **by** ten per cent in the last two years.

7 I don't think that Mr Gardener is prejudiced **at** / **against** any of the students, he's very fair.

8 John is really interested **for** / **in** German history, he knows so much!

9 Mark will throw a big party **at** / **on** Friday evening.

10 Did you know that Mrs Sutter is married **to** / **with** a Swiss man?

3 GRAMMAR REVISION + Talking about a school shop

____ / 6

There is a discussion at King's School about a school shop that should be run by students only. Mary is for the school shop, Monica is against it. Complete their arguments with the correct verb from the box.

will be able to • will do • will help • won't be able to • won't spend • won't work

Mary	Monica
The shop ______________________ students to work together.	The shop ______________________ because students buy their school things in the supermarket.
If you have forgotten an exercise book, you ______________________ buy it at school.	The students ______________________ their free time working in the shop. They will only work there during school hours.
The students ______________________ something useful in their free time.	The students ______________________ sell things cheaply enough.

4 GRAMMAR REVISION + Talking about the future

____ / 11

Über die Zukunft sprechen – welche Zeit muss ich verwenden?

- Du möchtest ausdrücken, dass etwas für die Zukunft geplant ist?
  ▸ *going to-future*
- Du möchtest ausdrücken, wie etwas in der Zukunft sein wird?
  ▸ *will-future*
- Du möchtest ausdrücken, dass etwas für die Zukunft fest verabredet ist?
  ▸ *present progressive*

Wenn du dir noch unsicher bist, lies noch einmal im Grammar File 5 auf S. 165 in deinem Englischbuch nach. Dort findest du weitere Beispiele.

a) *Complete the sentences with the* ***going to-future***, ***will-future*** *or* ***present progressive***. *(8P)*

1 Look, here is the ticket for my flight. I ______________________ (fly) to Spain tomorrow.

2 Lisa has just given me a call. I think she ______________________ (be) late for dinner.

3 I'm sorry, mum. I haven't had time to tidy up my room. I ______________________ (do) it after school. I promise!

4 Nick's just told me about his problems at school. We ______________________ (talk) to the teachers in a few days.

5 It's terribly cold, isn't it? But it ______________________ (be) warmer next week.

6 It's Sue's birthday in a few days. I ______________________ (send) her a nice birthday card.

7 We've already booked our holidays for next year. We ______________________ (go) to Florida again.

8 This year Susanna was chosen to play the main part in the school theatre production. I'm sure that next year it ______________________ (be) you, Alice.

b) *Now write three sentences about the future. Use the* ***going to-future***, ***will-future*** *and* ***present progressive***. *(3P)*

1 ____

2 ____

3 ____

5 GRAMMAR REVISION + About Ann's presentation

_____ /9

Adjective or adverb – kurze Wiederholung
Das Adjektiv erklärt näher, wie etwas oder jemand ist: **He is clever.**
Das Adverb erklärt näher, wie etwas gemacht wird: **He solved the problem cleverly.**

a) *Complete the sentences with words from the box. Decide if you need an* ***adjective*** *or an* ***adverb*** *and complete the sentences with the correct form. Be careful: there are two more than you need. (6P)*

careful • easy • equal • fantastic • good • nervous • personal • simple

1 I think she was a bit ______________________.

2 She had prepared her presentation

______________________.

3 Ann talked in a way that I could follow her presentation

______________________.

4 ______________________, I liked the way she kept looking at the audience.

5 The outline was worked out ______________________.

6 The photos she showed were ______________________.

b) *Finish the sentences. Write down whether you have to use an* ***adjective*** *or an* ***adverb****. (3P)*

1 The presentation was ______________________. (ad__________)

2 She talked too ______________________. (ad__________)

3 I think people liked listening because the topic was so ______________________. (ad__________)

MEDIATION

____/11

Have your say on Highway 2A

Im Unterricht behandelt ihr das Thema Bürgerbeteiligung. Du hast diesen Artikel über ein Bürgerbeteiligungs-projekt in Australien online gefunden und möchtest in der Schule darüber berichten.

Gib folgende Informationen auf deutsch wieder:

1 *Was die Verkehrsbehörde und die Gemeinde tun.*
2 *Worüber die Bürger befragt werden.*
3 *In welcher Form das Treffen stattfindet.*
4 *Wie die Bürger sich anmelden können.*
5 *Wie sich Bürger noch beteiligen können. (2 Fakten)*
6 *Wie die Bürger vorinformiert wurden. (3 Fakten)*

Road Services (RMS) are doing a report on the safety of Highway 2A at the moment.

Our citizens can have their say on the dangers of Highway 2A as part of a community workshop on Friday.

The community workshop forms part of the Northern Highway Road Safety review, and will be held between 10.30 am and 12.30 pm at Bay Waters Inn.

To register for the workshop, call Aretha on (067) 8866 5915. Roads Services (RMS) have said the phone number for residents wanting to register is now active.

People can also comment online using a special tool to show the locations where there are possible dangers, and make comments by emailing vista@highwayproject.com.

Notices were given to households along the Northern Highway, advertising the public meeting, and noting the phone number to register.

SPEAKING

____/ 21

12 At the end of school

Mittelberg Schule has asked its year 10 students to have their say about their school.
Listen to Paul talking about his six years at Mittelberg Schule.

Now you

You are leaving school soon. Have your say about your school.

Talk about

- *How it felt when you started at this school:*
  - *Were you excited, worried, happy?*
  - *What did you like about school, what didn't you like?*
- *How did your school life go on in years seven and eight?*
  - *Was it the same as in the years before?*
  - *What changed?*
- *How were your last two years? Talk about*
  - *your aims*
  - *success*
  - *bad times*
  - *the last few months at school*
- *At the end sum up your time at school and, if possible, give some advice on how the school should develop. Are there any tips you would like to give younger students?*

How to do well in a test

Countdown zum Testerfolg

Ein Test ist angekündigt? Kein Grund zur Panik. Wichtig ist, dass du weißt, worauf du dich vorbereiten musst. Im Zweifelsfall frag deine Lehrerin oder deinen Lehrer. Der Countdown kann beginnen!

Eine Woche vor dem Test

1 Lies noch einmal die **Texte** der zuletzt durchgenommenen Unit (A-Section und Text, eventuell auch das Background File). Fasse mündlich oder schriftlich zusammen, worum es ging.

2 Wiederhole den **Wortschatz** der Unit mit Hilfe des *Vocabulary* oder des *Wordmaster*. Schreibe dir die Wörter und Wortverbindungen, die du immer wieder vergisst, auf ein Blatt Papier. Eine Mindmap oder ein Wortfeld helfen beim Behalten.

3 Geh auch noch mal die neue **Grammatik** durch. Aufgaben zur Selbstüberprüfung und zum Üben findest du im *Practice*-Teil, auf der Seite „How am I doing?“, im *Grammar File* (S. 158–177), in deinem *Workbook* und im *e-Workbook*.

Zwei Tage vor dem Test

1 Wiederhole den **Wortschatz**. Manche Wörter sitzen noch nicht? Schreibe einen kurzen Text, in dem du sie verwendest.

2 Lies die **Texte** ein weiteres Mal.

3 Erkläre einem Freund oder einer Freundin die neue **Grammatik**. Das klappt nicht richtig? Dann lies nochmal im *Grammar File* nach.

Am Abend vor dem Test

1 Entspanne dich. Du kannst lesen, dich in die Badewanne legen, Musik hören, fernsehen, ...

2 Geh zur gewohnten Zeit ins Bett.

Am Morgen des Tests

1 Steh rechtzeitig auf, damit du nicht hetzen musst.

2 Lies irgendetwas „zum Aufwärmen“, aber schau nicht mehr in dein Schülerbuch.

Während des Tests

1 Denk daran: Du hast dich gut vorbereitet. Es gibt keinen Grund, nervös zu sein.

2 Konzentriere dich auf den Test, lass dich nicht ablenken.

3 Lies dir die Aufgaben genau durch. Dann löse zuerst die Aufgaben, die dir einfach scheinen. Wende dich erst danach den schwereren Aufgaben zu.

4 Aufgaben, die du bearbeitet hast, hakst du ab. So siehst du, wie du vorankommst, und behältst den Überblick.

5 Schau ab und zu auf die Uhr. Du solltest dir für den Schluss noch etwas Zeit einplanen, um deine Antworten noch einmal durchzulesen und wenn nötig zu korrigieren.

Aufgabenstellungen verstehen

Bevor du anfängst, die Aufgaben zu bearbeiten, vergewissere dich, dass du genau weißt, was du tun sollst. Lies die Aufgabe Wort für Wort langsam und gründlich und von Anfang bis Ende durch. Du kannst besonders wichtige Teile der Aufgabenstellung unterstreichen und die Aufgabe, wenn nötig, für dich in einzelne Schritte unterteilen.

Den folgenden Arbeitsanweisungen begegnest du häufig:

Add Verbinde eine Information oder einen Sachverhalt mit einer/einem anderen auf die geforderte Art und Weise.

Choose Wähle zwischen verschiedenen Möglichkeiten die passende Information aus.

Comment Kommentiere einen Sachverhalt durch die Darstellung deiner eigenen Meinung dazu. Begründe und erläutere sie möglichst genau.

Compare Vergleiche Dinge, Wörter oder Sachverhalte, indem du prüfst, ob und auf welche Weise sie gleiche oder verschiedene Eigenschaften, Aussehen, Bedeutungen oder Funktionen haben.

Complete Ergänze eine Information, indem du sie an dem dafür vorgesehenen Platz einträgst und damit z. B. einen Satz sinnvoll beendest.

Describe Beschreibe ein Objekt oder eine Person, d.h. stelle dar, wie sie aussehen, wie das Objekt funktioniert oder die Personen handeln. Vermeide eigene Wertungen wie z. B. „beautiful“, „useful“ oder „great“.

Discuss Diskutiere ein Thema, eine Behauptung oder eine Aussage. Untersuche möglichst viele Seiten davon, z. B. Vor- und Nachteile, und stelle diese geordnet dar.

Explain Erkläre einen Sachverhalt, d. h. gib wesentliche Fakten über ihn und erläutere, wie sie logisch zusammenhängen.

Fill in Trage die geforderten Informationen in den dafür vorgesehenen Platz ein, z. B. in eine Lücke oder eine Tabelle.

List Schreibe einzelne oder mehrere Informationen übersichtlich und geordnet auf, z. B. in einer Reihe, Tabelle oder einem anderen Verzeichnis.

Listen Höre dir einen Text, einzelne Informationen oder Sachverhalte an.

Match Ordne die angegebenen Informationen einander zu, wie es die Aufgabe erfordert. Finde z. B. Satzanfänge und passende Satzenden und füge sie zusammen.

Use Verwende eine Tatsache, ein Wort usw. so, wie es in der Aufgabe gefordert wird.

Write a ... Schreibe etwas in einem geforderten Textformat auf, z. B. deinen Kommentar zu etwas oder eine Geschichte.

D6 Erweiterte Ausgabe

English G 21

Klassenarbeitstrainer

für Schülerinnen und Schüler

Lösungen und Lerntipps

Cornelsen

LISTENING

01 1 A radio phone-in – today's topic: How did you meet your partner?

Presenter Good morning and a very warm welcome to the show! Today we're going to be talking about the wonderful topic of "love". We want to know: Where did you meet your husband, wife, boyfriend or girlfriend? So call in and tell us the story of the love of your life!

– Great, we have our first caller. Good morning Lisa. We're very excited to hear your story. Where did you meet your man?

Lisa Oh, hi. Good morning, John. Well, I think my story is very romantic. It was the day before my 20th birthday. It was a pretty stressful day because I'd planned a big party but I hadn't bought anything for it yet. So after work I went straight to the supermarket and threw everything into a shopping basket. But guess what happened when I was at the cash desk and wanted to pay? I realized that I didn't have any money with me! I was so embarrassed! You know, this all happened 25 years ago when credit cards weren't very common yet ... I had everything packed in my bags already and the queue behind me was getting longer and longer. I didn't have the time to leave my shopping there and come back because I had to go straight to my evening classes. And then suddenly, the young man behind me offered to pay for my shopping. It was so lovely of him! And he didn't ask for anything from me in return, he just said he was sure I would pay him back later. So he gave me his business card with his address on it and wrote his bank details on it. That was all. I was so lucky! I took my shopping and went to my classes. The next morning I bought a bottle of wine and went to the young man's home. I gave him the money and invited him to my birthday party. We had a wonderful evening and started dating. Well, yes, what can I say? We fell in love and got married three years later. We've been married ever since, have three wonderful children and, yes, of course, we sometimes fight, but we're still very happy. So, there you have it – that's my story!

Presenter What a wonderful and romantic story, Lisa! Thank you for sharing it with us.

Lerntipp **Notizen machen während des Anhörens**

Finde heraus, welche Methode des Mitschreibens für dich am besten passt. Du kannst mit einer Mindmap arbeiten oder Stichworte aufschreiben. Auf jeden Fall solltest du Daten (Wochentage, Jahr, ...) oder Zahlen (Preise, ...), die in einem Text vorkommen, für dich schriftlich festhalten.

a)

1 Lisa talks about	a) her birthday and the day before.	✔
	b) her 20th birthday.	
	c) a man in her evening classes.	
	d) her birthday presents.	

2 The young man	a) used his credit card.	
	b) didn't want to have the money back.	
	c) was standing behind Lisa.	✔
	d) wanted to go to Lisa's party.	

3 Lisa and the young man	a) drank a bottle of French wine together.	
	b) started going out after her party.	✔
	c) want to get married soon.	
	d) want to have at least three children.	

4 After Lisa's story, the reporter says that	a) another person is going to tell their story.	
	b) there is a break now.	
	c) he liked the story.	✔
	d) they are going to play a love song.	

02 *Presenter* And now we have Nick on the line. Hello, Nick. You have a bit of a heartbreaking story for us, right?

Nick Yes, mmh, hi. I wanted to tell the story about my first love.

Presenter OK, great, go on then.

Nick Well, yeah. It was the beginning of year ten at school. There was a new girl in our class. She was from London and she was pretty! You know, I was at school in Bristol, and we thought she was so cool! All the boys in my class fancied her and we did many really stupid things to get her to notice us. You know, all that teenage stuff like writing letters, recording cassettes with the latest love songs, acting all cool and trying to look like we didn't care about anything when really we were like jelly inside! You know, stupid teenage stuff. To be honest, I never thought I'd have a chance with her because, well, I'm pretty average-looking. But I was lucky because one weekend I went to a course on how to apply for jobs and to my surprise she was there as well. I was impressed because I hadn't thought she was interested in stuff like that ... But, anyway, we had a lot of fun together. We didn't know anyone else on the course so we worked as a pair on all the tasks for the whole day. Afterwards we went out for a drink. We had a great evening and other dates followed, you know. That was the beginning of a wonderful love story. We were together for four years before we broke up. That was ten years ago now. She got married since then, as did I, but we still have contact by email.

Presenter Thanks, Nick. That was a little sad somehow but still a great story, thank you. Hope your wife isn't jealous ...

Nick Haha, no, there's no need for that!

Presenter Well, then, thanks for calling! – And now, anybody else wanting to tell the listeners their romantic story? Call us! We're back after some music to chat with the next caller.

b)

1 in London

2 wrote letters, recorded cassettes with love songs, tried to look cool

3 on a course

4 because they didn't know the others

5 four years

6 they are in contact by email

03 *Presenter* Hi everyone and welcome back. We're talking about great love stories today. So, Anna has a wonderful multicultural story for us. Hi Anna, share it with us!

Anna Haha, hi John. Well, I got to know my boyfriend when my cousin got married two months ago. My cousin lives in Germany and her boyfriend – or husband – is from England. They had their party in a nice restaurant outside Harrogate. Of course, there were also lots of Germans there, and they wanted to make sure the guests all chatted with each other, so they placed German and English people next to each other so that never two neighbours were from the same country. A lot of the Germans spoke really good English but others didn't at all. A boy about my age, I'm 17, was sitting next to me. He was very sweet but we had some trouble talking to each other because well, he didn't really speak English and, umm, my German isn't very good either.
So, as you can imagine, at first it was pretty hard and we just sat there for ages! But he seemed really nice so I tried really hard to find a topic that we could talk about. After a while we got onto films and that was the ice breaker! Not that we could suddenly talk to each other perfectly or anything, but it was way better than before. We found we liked the same kinds of films and had the same sense of humour, so we made a date to go to the cinema the next day. And I swear – we had the best time ever! I've never had as much fun as I did that evening. It was such a great date and we spent loads of time together the week he was in England. I really felt like we were falling in love by the end of the week.

Presenter And then what happened?

Anna Yeah, well then he had to go back to Germany because he's training to be a chef. I still go to college here in England but I'm finishing in the summer. After that I want to go to Germany and learn his language. I just want to be near him! And I think that's what he wants too.
I don't know how the whole thing is going to turn out, but I hope we'll end up as a happy family.

Presenter Oh, wow, Anna, very romantic. Thank you! We all wish you lots of luck!

c)

1 Anna got to know her boyfriend <u>two months ago at her cousin's wedding</u>.
2 Her cousin is from Germany, and her husband <u>is from England</u>.
3 Anna sat next to <u>a German boy</u>.
4 The German boy <u>didn't speak English very well</u>.
5 Their conversation got better when they <u>started to talk about films</u>.
6 On the day after the wedding party <u>they went to see a film together</u>.
7 When Anna has finished college, she <u>wants to go to Germany</u>.

04 ***Presenter*** Right, the next caller is on the line: Leo. He's only 18 but already completely in love. So, hi Leo. Where did you meet your lovely lady?

Leo Hi John, I'm so excited to be on the radio! OK, so here's my story: a while ago I started going to dancing classes at a local club with a friend of mine. I know that sounds pretty stupid, but my mate is such a good dancer, and he told me I needed to work on my moves a bit, as girls really like a good dancer. We were really lucky, because the class had way more girls than boys in it, so it was easy to find a dance partner – yeah, it was pretty cool to be able to pick and choose! Haha. Anyway, so I danced – or well, I tried to dance – with different girls but it is way harder than it looks on TV, I can tell you! I couldn't remember all the steps and I kept messing up, treading on the girls' toes and all that. Pretty embarrassing ... Anyway, there was one really sweet girl there but I didn't get to talk to her much because I had to concentrate on the dance steps, and at the end of the class she disappeared so I never got to chat her up. Actually, I think I was just happy it was the end of the class by that point! I never wanted to go back again, but I couldn't get this girl out of my head, so I ended up going again the next week. And that time I asked her on a date at the end of the class! That was six months ago, and now we are completely in love but I haven't tried to dance since then! She really wants me to go to the dance class with her again and it's her birthday coming up next week, so I was thinking I might take her there as a surprise. I'll see ...

Presenter Great idea! Be brave, young man, and surprise her! Thanks for your story and say hello to your girlfriend. You can practise dancing to the next song, Leo. Well, I hope all you listeners are feeling romantic too. That's the end of our phone in. Thanks for sharing all your stories! Next up, we're talking about the latest films coming out at the cinema. Don't miss it!

d)

	right	wrong
1 Leo had invited a friend to a dancing club.		✔
2 There were more boys than girls.		✔
3 Leo talked a lot to the nice girl.		✔
4 Leo had some problems with dancing.	✔	
5 Perhaps Leo will go to the classes again.	✔	

e)

Mögliche Lösungen:

1 A friend had invited Leo to a dancing club.

2 There were more girls than boys.

3 Leo didn't talk to the girl a lot because he had to concentrate on the steps.

05 2 At the café

Catherine Um, excuse me. Is this seat taken or do you mind if I sit at your table?

Jonathan Oh no, of course not. Sit down, please.

Catherine Thank you. Could I have a look through the job advertisements in your newspaper? Or were you still going to read it?

Jonathan No sure, take it. What job are you looking for? Oh, sorry: I'm Jonathan.

Catherine Hi Jonathan, I'm Catherine. Nice to meet you. Oh, I'm just looking for a part time job – anything really. To make a bit of extra money, you know.

Jonathan Oh, yeah, I know what you mean. What have you done so far?

Catherine Well, I've just finished school, but my results are only average. I really want to go to art school but I have to hand in some examples of my art work to get a place at the college. So I need to work on my paintings and drawings for the next few months. And I need equipment, which is really, really expensive. So that's why I need the job. What about you?

Jonathan I finished school last year and at the moment I'm training to be a mechanic in a little garage near here.

Catherine Really? That's cool. And do you like your job? How did you get into mechanics?

Jonathan Yeah, I love the job. I'm really happy to have it as well, because it's a good chance to prepare for technical college. It's a lot of work every day but I'm learning lots of things there. I already know a lot about cars and now I can repair my father's car, which is pretty cool. I want to have a car of my own so I need to save money every week for that. But I'm not saving that much, because I also want to have a life, you know? Go out with friends, party, all that kind of stuff. So, I really know what you are talking about with your art school and the job. Life's really expensive. Do you still live with your parents?

Catherine Yeah, I do. That makes things a bit easier.

Jonathan So, is this going to be your first job then or have you had another job before?

Catherine No, it isn't. I worked as a waitress in a little café before. But it was nowhere near as busy as this one and it was a bit boring working there and after six months I needed a change. After that I worked in a mobile phone shop but that wasn't for me. I like texting my mates and calling people on my mobile but that's not all I'm interested in.

Jonathan So what job are you looking for now?

Catherine Yeah, well, that's exactly the problem: I don't know where to look for a job. It's so hard and I'm getting really down about it. Do you have any suggestions?

→

Jonathan Umm, let me think. Why don't you try a supermarket or a bookshop? You could pop in directly and ask if they need help. Or maybe in a hospital? Or, hey, a friend of mine works in a travel agency, and she says it's really fun.

Catherine That sounds great! Thanks for the ideas. I think I'll definitely try the travel agencies.

Jonathan Cool. Oh, sorry I've really got to get back to work, my break's over. It was nice talking to you though. And well, maybe we could meet up again sometime?

Catherine Sure, I'd like that. Then I can tell you all about my brilliant career! You can call me if you like. I'll give you my number. It's 07894 …

a)

A 8, B 1, C 3, D 4, E 2, F 5, G 7, H 6

b)

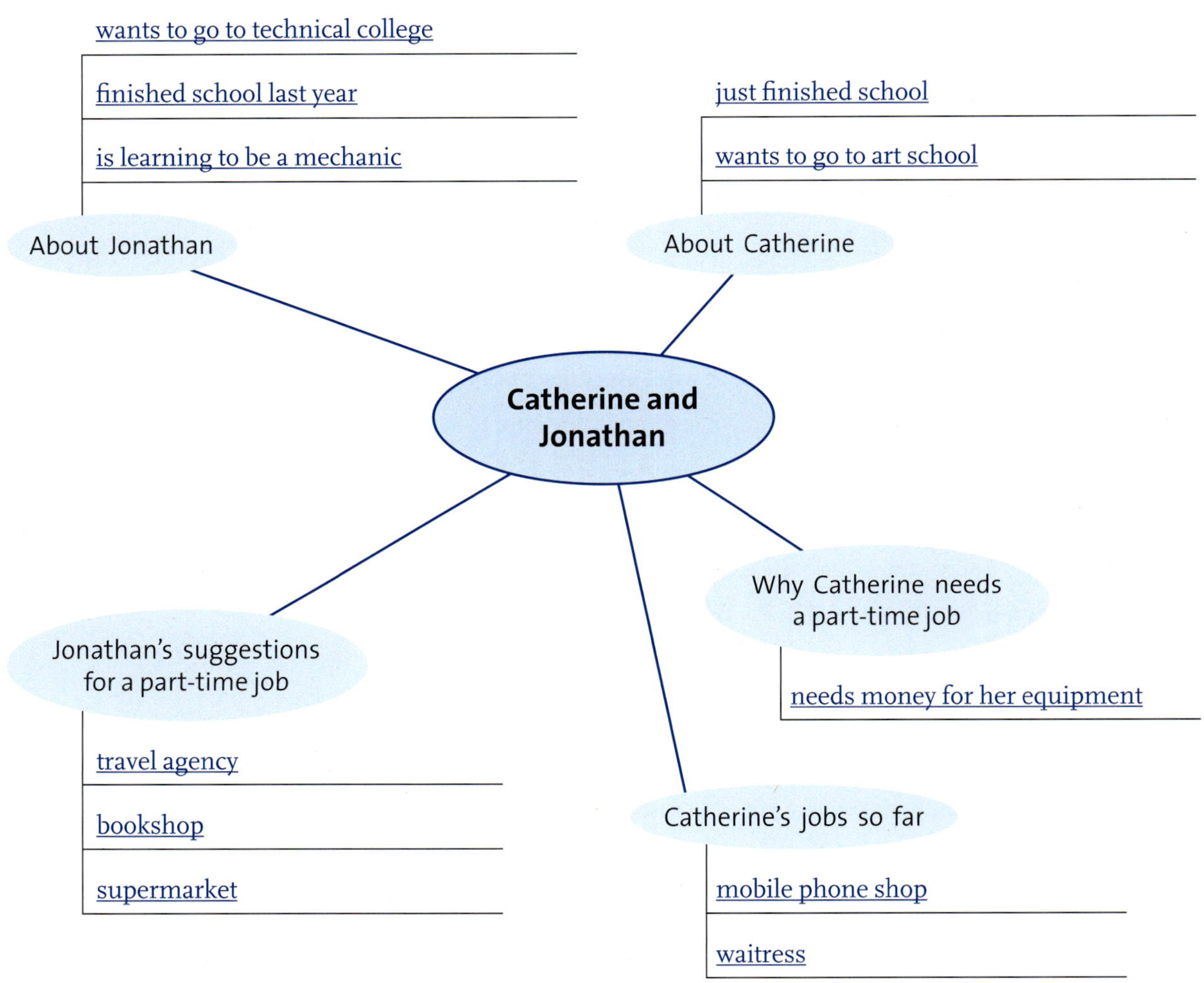

LANGUAGE

1 WORDS Me and my friends

I have many friends, boys and girls. Their appearance is different. Most of them are quite thin, some have straight hair, only three of them have curly hair. Some of the girls are really good-looking and attractive.
I don't like arrogant people, so of course all of them are really charming.
Ah, you want to know some things about me too? Well, I think I'm a lovable person with a good sense of humour. I don't like working so much so some people say that I'm lazy. But I laugh a lot and I always talk to people in a friendly way. And I should also mention that I make friends with people easily and that I like to flirt with the girls.

Lösungswort für die blue boxes: loyal

2 GRAMMAR REVISION + My friends and their hobbies

Mara, one of my friends, loves taking photos. She always carries her camera around. She doesn't take any photos of people, she always takes photos of nature. Here you can see her. She is taking a photo of a flower.
Susan loves languages. At the moment she is learning Dutch. She speaks English, Spanish and Italian.
She doesn't speak Portuguese but she also wants to learn German.
Here you can see Philip, Chris and Ava. They don't like watching TV, in fact one of them even hates it.
Sometimes they watch a film at the cinema. In this photo they are playing one of their many board games.

3 GRAMMAR REVISION + A social day for Mike and his friends

a)

"We had decided to join the 'Community Day' long before the actual day. We simply wanted to do something for our town. And we thought it would be fun working together. It was our job to clean places inside and outside town. We started at the station where we didn't find a lot of rubbish. We were more successful when we went to the small river near our town.
We found many different things: a lot of rubbish like paper, plastic and glasses, of course, but also a mobile phone, a watch and an old school-bag. After we had taken away all the rubbish, we tried to find the owner of the mobile phone. As we weren't successful in finding him or her, we took it to the lost property office. In the evening we were invited to an Italian restaurant by the mayor of our town."

b)

had decided, had taken

I use the past perfect when I want to show that something had happened before another action in the past.

Mögliche Lösungen:

1 After I had done my homework I watched a film.

2 Pete went to France when he had passed his exam.

3 They had taken their seats before the others arrived.

Lerntipp **Simple past und past perfect – unregelmäßige Verben**

- Für die Bildung dieser zwei Zeiten musst du sicher in den unregelmäßigen Verben sein.
- Noch einmal zur Erinnerung: Das **simple past** wird mit der 2. Form und das **past perfect** wird mit **had** plus der 3. Form des Verbs gebildet.
- Wiederhole daher die unregelmäßigen Verben. Du findest sie in deinem Englischbuch auf S. 224–225.

MEDIATION

Ein Freund, ein guter Freund

Mögliche Lösungen:

1 The topic of the festival is "good friends". The film should be about a friend who is always there for you and helps you in difficult situations. In the film, you can show a situation where your friend has problems with his parents and how you can help him or her. Another idea is that you make a film about problems at school, e.g. when you are bullied. (4P)

2 You can send in a complete short film or an idea for a film or a cartoon. (3P)

3 You have to send it in by February 1st, the film mustn't be longer than four minutes and you mustn't be older than 14. (3P)

4 There are teenagers and adults in the jury. The winning film will be shown at the national film festival in October. The winner of the second place will get 150 euros as a price, the winner of the third place will get 100 euros. (4P)

WRITING

How I got to know ...

Mögliche Lösung:

Two years ago my marks for Maths became very bad. So my parents sent me to evening classes especially for Maths. I didn't want to go there but I had to. (3P)

And that's where I met Pete. He was a student at the evening classes too. I liked him from the first moment. (3P) He was in the same situation as me. But he really wanted to become better. I liked him for this. It helped me with my Maths. (4P) We both started to believe in ourselves, we even learned Maths together. (2P)

And with the help of the young teacher we started to like Maths and became better within a short period of time. Pete and I became very good friends and we still are today. (4P)

READING

YFC – Young Film Competition

1 12–22
2 no
3 no
4 during four weekends in January and February
5 at the film festival
6 yes, the three best will get awards
7 write an email to the given address
8 10th October
9 from the archive
10 on the homepage, see FAQs

LANGUAGE

1 WORDS About films

1 Timothy works as a reviewer and writes about films for a famous film magazine.
2 Sometimes films are different from the books that they are based on.
3 Susan likes films with friendship and love, she likes romantic films.
4 People who are interested in history like films that are set in previous centuries.
5 Even if you don't like the story of a film, you might like the special effects and the costume of the main actress.
6 The Oscar is the most famous film award.
7 I have just seen a great new film at the cinema. You should go and see it. I bet you will like it just as much I do.
8 Pete wants to see this new film that stars Brad Pitt.
9 Next week we are going to the cinema together with our teacher. The film is called "Let's go Green". The topic is our environment.

2 WORDS Getting by in English

1 I don't like coffee. I'd like tea instead.
2 I didn't catch your name.
3 Ann is very arrogant unlike her brother Adam who is very charming.
4 Julie is six months pregnant.

3 GRAMMAR REVISION + A survey on young people

Mögliche Lösungen:

1 No, she doesn't. She does her homework on Monday, Tuesday and Wednesday.

2 Linn usually meets her friends at the weekend.

3 Dave plays computer games twice a week.

4 Joe often does sports.

5 Joe and Dave never learn German vocabulary.

6 No, he doesn't. He helps his parents on Saturday.

7 Dave and Linn both always do their homework on Monday.

4 GRAMMAR REVISION + What will be in the future?

Interviewer We now have the chance to talk to one of our young film-makers here ... So, Joanna, thank you for the exciting film about the two friends. Now, let's talk a bit about your future. What can you tell us about it?

Joanna Well, I hope I will have the chance to make many more films in the future, so that I will be able to learn more about filmmaking. I hope I will go to a film academy in the near future.

Interviewer We will be glad to see more of your films. I'm sure you will make other exciting films and will be able to go to the film acadamy. Are there any topics you are especially interested in and are there others you are not interested in, Joanna?

Joanna Well, I can definitely say I will not make any detective stories because I'm interested in crime stories. I suppose I will go on making films about relationships, I think this is something people are always interested in.

Interviewer Many people will be happy to hear about your plans for more films. I'm sure you will become famous.

Joanna Thanks very much. I hope so too.

Interviewer Thank you and goodbye.

5 GRAMMAR REVISION + My ideas for the film

I had the idea for "Her Eyes" when I was in the swimming pool last summer. Suddenly I saw this girl who wasn't particularly pretty but her eyes were special. But I didn't talk to her. After I had left the swimming pool, I still thought about her eyes and started making up a love story. First I didn't write down anything, I just thought of ideas. But because I hadn't written down my ideas, I soon forgot them. So I decided to write them on small pieces of paper. That was a really good idea. After about three weeks I had collected all my ideas and I then wrote down everything. The film was produced this year in February.

Lerntipp **Verwendung des past perfect**

- Überlege noch einmal, warum an den drei Stellen in der obenstehenden Aufgabe das **past perfect** verwendet werden muss.
- Bilde weitere Sätze, in denen man das **past perfect** verwenden muss.
- So kannst du dir am einfachsten darüber klar werden, wie es verwendet wird.

6 GRAMMAR REVISION + A backstage meeting

Mögliche Lösungen:

At what age did you decide to become an actor?

Were the years before you became a star difficult?

Do you still like your job?

What are your plans for the future?

Do you already know the title of your next film?

What would you advise a person who wants to become an actor?

Lerntipp **Bildung von Fragen**

- Das Grammar File 2 auf S. 161 in deinem Englischbuch listet verschiedene Möglichkeiten der Fragebildung auf.
- Nutze es, wann immer du Fragen bilden willst (außer natürlich bei Klassenarbeiten in der Schule!)
- Du kannst dir selbst weitere solche Aufgaben stellen: Überlege dir eine Person (aus dem Freundeskreis, berühmte Stars oder Politiker) und überlege dir Fragen, die du dieser Person stellen möchtest.
- Überprüfe deine Fragen anhand des Lösungsvorschlags zu dieser Aufgabe und des Grammar File 2.
- Hole dir beim Überprüfen auch immer mal wieder Hilfe von deinem Lehrer/deiner Lehrerin oder einer anderen Person, die gut Englisch spricht.

MEDIATION

Almanya – Willkommen in Deutschland

Mögliche Lösung:

Six-year-old Cenk Yilmaz doesn't know if he is German or Turkish. (1P) His cousin Canan tells him his grandfather's story. (1P) His grandfather Hüseyin came to Germany as a Turkish worker in the 1960s. Later the whole family came to Germany, too. (2P) Canan talks about their life in Germany and about their dreams and the many problems they had in the foreign country. (3P) One evening the grandfather has a surprise for the whole family. He has bought a house in Turkey for their holidays. (2P) The whole family travels to Turkey. (1P) During the journey they remember things from the past. (1P)

In the end, something surprising happens during their journey and Cenk gets a very special job. (2P)

SPEAKING

06 An interview with a young film-maker

Luke Let's talk about the beginning of your film career. How did you get the idea of making a film when you were only 17?

Neil Well, when I was a child I loved going to the cinema with my dad. And then we did a project about films at school where we even produced some short scenes. I think that was the beginning.

Luke And then at 15 you started with "My Wave". It's a film about young people's lives, their happy moments, but also about their sad moments with a lot of problems. Where did you get the inspiration for the film from?

Neil Hm, some parts describe moments from my own life, but for many others parts I got the inspiration from people I watched, also from my friends of course.

Luke Did you want to give a message to the audience of your film?

Neil When I made the film, I didn't think about messages. But today I'm sure that my film does give a message to young people. It's quite easy really: don't give up even if you face a lot of problems, try to see things positively and talk about your problems.

Luke You also played a role in your film. How did you do that? It was probably very difficult to direct the film and to act at the same time.

Neil It definitely was difficult, sometimes I had problems managing. But I think it is important to understand the two different roles and to see them as two separate jobs. And, of course, you have to be honest with yourself and your own acting.

Luke What did a normal day look like for you?

Neil The days of the production were really hard work because we worked for 10 sometimes even 12 hours a day and we did this 6 days a week.

Luke This doesn't sound romantic at all. Were there moments when you thought, 'oh I wish I hadn't started with this film'?

Neil Oh no, I loved this work too much to have thoughts like that although it was hard work.

Luke Are you working on another film at the moment?

Neil No, I'm not, I'm having a break right now. I need time to think about further projects.

Luke Sounds as if you already have ideas for the future. Will you make another film?

Neil Definitely yes, I will.

Luke Can you tell us about your plans?

Neil I'd like to make a film about bullying at school. But this needs a lot of research before I can start working on the film.

Luke Well that just leaves us to wish you all the best for your future work. And – we are looking forward to more of your films. Thank you for the interview.

Neil You're welcome.

Now you

Mögliche Lösung:

You	Let's talk about the making of your film "Old Mrs Creek's dog". How did you get the idea for this film? (2P)
Your partner	This is a funny story. My grandmother has a dog and she doesn't talk to many people during the day but to her dog. This is a bit strange but she is very happy and I thought this could make a funny film.
You	That's really interesting. What is the film about? Can you tell us a bit about the content? (3P)
Your partner	As the title says, it's about an old woman and her dog. It shows the normal day of an old lady who lives alone in a small house and she only speaks to her dog. It is about the relationship between them.
You	Making the film must have been funny. Can you tell us a bit about it? (2P)
Your partner	Yes, sure. The grandmother is my own grandmother and she liked it very much. She loved being the main actor in the film. And the dog is her own dog. This was rather difficult because the dog often didn't do what we wanted him to do.
You	Yes, I see what you mean. Are there only those two characters in the film? (1P)
Your partner	Yes, it's only granny and her dog.
You	OK. Another thing I would like to ask you: What about your future? Do you already have any plans for the future? (3P)
Your partner	Well, I'm only 12 years old so I don't have real plans for the future. At the moment it's only school, school, school. But I love animals very much, maybe I'll become a vet some day.
You	OK. Good luck for your future and thank you for your funny film! Bye. (2P)
Your partner	Thank you. Bye.

Lerntipp **So kannst du Speaking üben**

Du kannst den Dialog auch noch einmal mit dem anderen Filmplakat üben.
Wenn du möchtest, können du und dein Partner/deine Partnerin bei einem weiteren Durchgang auch die Rollen tauschen.

Lösungen A

READING

1 Teenagers and the media

a)

Mögliche Lösungen:

1 Name two things about teenagers and TV.	– they (many of them) say they can do without it more than without their mobile – they watch more TV than ever		
2 Give the percentage of children from lower classes who don't have access to the internet at home.	20 %		
3 Name two things teenagers use the internet for.	education, entertainment		
4 Write down the percentage of children who would miss their mobile, the internet and the TV this year and last year.		this year	last year
	mobile	28 %	31 %
	internet	25 %	24 %
	TV	18 %	24 %
5 Write down the number of teenagers who listen to the radio.	about half of them		
6 Name the place in the house where most children use the internet.	living room		
7 Write down percentage increase in children with a smartphone from last year to this year.	10 %		

b)

1 Not all children have internet access.

2 The annual survey was carried out in spring this time.

3 More parents care about how their children's use of the internet.

4 Many of the younger children use the internet together with an adult in the room.

5 More than half of the children aged 8–11 use a mobile.

Lerntipp **Unbekannte Wörter erschließen**

- Lies dir noch einmal den Handhinweis vor dem Lesetext dieser Klassenarbeit genau durch.
- Trainiere das Erschließen unbekannter Wörter so oft es geht. Das kann im Unterricht mit einem unbekannten Text sein oder auch Zuhause, wenn du einen Text im Internet liest.

2 A do-it-yourself workshop

a)

1 Customers come to the bike workshop	a) when they are looking for a new bike.	
	b) when they have a problem with their bike.	✔
	c) when they are looking for somebody to repair their bike.	

2 Bike workshops	a) can also be found in other cities.	✔
	b) are always a big risk.	
	c) are run by people for their friends.	

3 Emma wasn't sure	a) if she really wanted a bike workshop.	
	b) if her friends would help to renovate the garage.	
	c) if she could earn enough money with the bike workshop.	✔

4 Henry	a) repairs the bikes.	
	b) thinks that people must get to know their bikes.	✔
	c) likes the atmosphere in the bike workshop.	

5 Emma is sure that	a) the bike workshop helps the environment.	✔
	b) everybody can make his or her individual bike with many different parts.	
	c) the author of the article will find the missing part he is looking for.	

6 Most of the customers	a) don't have much money.	
	b) would prefer to repair their bikes at home.	
	c) are a kind of bike fans.	✔

b)

Mögliche Lösungen:

What are the opening hours of the bike workshop?

When did you open the bike workshop?

How many customers do you have per day?

Would you like to open another bike workshop?

Do you earn enough money to live on it?

LANGUAGE

1 WORDS From the newspapers

1 Since 1970 British people need about 34% more energy. Use appliances that save energy!

2 The latest figures show that UK emissions fell by 7% in 2011.

3 Will Britain reach its targets and reduce its carbon footprint?

4 Because of the warm winter, less power was needed in Britain.

5 A Brighton high school student is proud of his new invention. Look at his solar barbecue.

6 The insulation of the town hall will cost more than expected.

7 Global warming is the most complicated environmental problem the world has to solve.

8 Greenhouse gases are mainly produced by burning fossil fuels.

9 The amount of carbon dioxide produced rose again.

2 WORDS A crossword

Across

1 power cut 7 conditions 8 pretend

Down

2 responsible 3 unplug 4 appliance 5 choice 6 no-no

3 GRAMMAR REVISION + My bike is repaired

a)

Adam Have you got a new bike? Your old one is broken, isn't it?

Oliver I wasn't able to afford a new one, so I repaired my old one.

Adam I don't believe it! Did you repair it yourself?

Oliver Yes, I did. I was able to do it with the help of the bike workshop down the road.

Adam Hey, it must be new. I haven't heard of it.

Oliver Yes, it is. It's great! I went there with my broken bike. A young man showed me round and then I was allowed to use all the tools they have.

Adam What about new parts?

Oliver Ah, good question. I didn't have to buy any new part. They supply hundreds of used parts and you simply look for the part you need. Of course you have to pay for it. I also had to pay for using the workshop at the end, but believe me, it was a fair price. I was able to pay it from my pocket-money.

b)

Mögliche Lösungen:

1 I'm able to go to school by bike.

2 I wasn't able to go by bike when I was four years old.

3 I'm not allowed to drive a car.

4 Last week my bike was broken so I had to go to school by bus.

5 Last week I had to repair my bike.

4 GRAMMAR REVISION + About the environmental projects

a)

	who	which	that	not necessary
1 The project were we plant trees is the project ____________ I like best.		✔	✔	✔
2 Look, there is the girl ____________ is in the same project as me.	✔		✔	
3 The head teacher is talking to the students of the project ____________ deals with the pollution of the air.		✔	✔	
4 Sue and Carmelita are the two girls ____________ I work with in my project.	✔		✔	✔
5 Alan is the one ____________ is responsible for painting the posters in his project.	✔		✔	

b)

Mögliche Lösungen:

1 Oliver is the boy who/that I got to know in my project.

2 Repairing old bikes is the project which/that I would like to choose.

3 The boy who/that rang up five minutes ago is in my project too.

WRITING

Gadgets on class trips

Our school rules say that we are not allowed to take mobile phones and MP3-players with us. (1P)
I think it is OK not to allow MP3-players. On a class trip, the whole class should be together and have fun together. When everybody just listens to his or her own music, we cannot be a team. (3P) But I don't think it is a good idea to leave our mobile phones at home. It can be very useful to have a mobile phone. On a day trip, for example, students are sometimes allowed to go somewhere in small groups. But what happens if they lose their way or if they are late? If some of them have a mobile with them, they can easily call the teacher. Maybe they are in a dangerous situation. Then they can also call the police. (4P)
I think they should change the rules and should allow the students to take their mobiles with them. Maybe it is a good idea to ban texting. (2P)

LISTENING

1 Talking about the environment

Host Hello and welcome back to the show all about our wonderful environment. Our listeners have called up with questions they'd like to ask and our expert Amanda Stokker is going to answer them. She's in the studio with me. Good morning Amanda.

Amanda Hi, good morning. It's great to be here.

Host It's great to have you here. We have a very interesting question from one of our listeners: Michael from Washington. He asks: "What's better for the environment: flying or driving?" So, Amanda, it's your turn now.

Amanda That is indeed an interesting question and the answer is simple: Let's say he wants to do a trip of about 300 miles. Going by car is better for the environment if you have quite a fuel-efficient, medium-sized car. Then driving produces about 104 kilograms of CO_2. Flying in a normal plane would produce about 184 kilograms of CO_2 per passenger.

Host Wow, that's a huge difference. How many passengers are in the car then?

Amanda Only one. Surprising isn't it? And of course, it would be even better if there were more than one person in the car: if you have four people in the car, it's still only 104 kilograms of CO_2 produced in total or 26 kilograms per person. If you compare that to a flight of 300 miles: the amount of CO_2 produced for four people on the flight is 736 kilograms! So you can see, driving in this case would be an easy way to do something for the environment.

Host Yes, it would be. But what about the price of the gas for the car and the cost of flights?

Amanda As we all know, gas prices are quite high. That's what makes driving far more expensive if you're going the same distance. So flying is cheaper, and that's exactly why many people prefer flying. Yeah, and umm, of course, flying also saves time as we probably all know. But if you're not travelling that far, going by car can still be faster. And once again: The more people are in the car, the cheaper it gets.

Host That makes sense. Now one last question: What about public transport?

Amanda Well, that's an even better way to get around, of course. CO_2 emissions are a lot lower when you take the bus or go by train. The only way to travel greener would be to go by bicycle or walking. That produces the lowest carbon footprint, which won't surprise you, but you're going to need pretty strong legs to do a 300 mile trip by foot or bike, right?

Host OK, thank you for answering Michael's question. Hope you got your answer, Michael. Next, we have another question for our expert Amanda Stokker. Rebecca from Burke wants to know ...

a)

One person in a car on a trip of 300 miles produces 104 kg CO_2.

Four people in a car on a trip of 300 miles produce 104 kg CO_2.

One person on a plane on a trip of 300 miles produces 184 kg CO_2.

Four people on a plane on a trip of 300 miles produce 736 kg CO_2.

b)

1 Many people prefer flying because it's cheaper and it saves time.

2 A longer trip by car can be cheaper than flying if there are more people in the car.

3 If you use public transport, emissions are a lot lower.

2 A family discussion

a)

Dad	Oh can you pass me the sugar there Sarah.
Sarah	Yeah, here you are. Could I have the milk, please?
Dad	Yeah, yeah, OK.
Dad	All right now, listen to this kids. I saw a leaflet. This is a car sharing scheme. It sounds really interesting. I don't know exactly what it costs but anyway, let me tell you the details.
Sarah	So you, wait, do you mean we gonna get rid of our car?
Dad	No, no, this's, just wait a moment. So first of all, we don't have to own a car, OK, just become a member of this scheme and they run lots of cars. There's cars parked at different places all over the city. You just book a car on the internet, you know, and you can and drive if it's available.
Sarah	How much is that gonna cost dad?
Dad	Well, that's the thing I don't yet know, Sarah, but anyway, just listen to the details, cause it sounds very interesting. Now; I had never thought about this before but I think it's really really interesting. I mean, first of all you help the environment. OK . And this you know, I think we should all try to make a difference. And we don't drive that much in a whole year here anyway, ...
Sarah	Yeah, but ...
Dad	We're on a bike ... Wait a minute. This would save money, it's keeping people fit, and we can use public transport, it's cheaper, we haven't got to pay tax, or insurance for the car. Now, I don't know what it costs yet, that's true, OK, but I have been thinking of selling the family car so cause we don't really need a car.
Chris, Sarah	But dad!

→

Chris But dad, we don't live in London, or any big city where we really have the opportunity to take public transportation or anything.

Sarah It's true!

Chris It's really difficult.

Sarah Having a car, that gives you freedom dad, you know. And next year I'm gonna be 17. and I was really looking forward to start to learn to drive.

Dad Don't you think there's enough cars in the world Sarah?

Dad Yeah, OK. But you havne't got to start, you haven't got a start right away. You can learn how to drive ... you're only 17.

Sarah Yeah, but, you know, if we have a car, then I can do lessons with you as well as with it, with an instructor and that's gonna save me a lot of money.

Dad Yes, I suppose you're right.

Sarah What about like, last week when I went to Rachel's party, and you picked me up at like midnight. Would you be able to do that with one of those car sharing cars?

Dad We can get a taxi if need need it.

Sarah Yeah, but ...

Dad There won't a be a party every week.

Sarah Then what about the shopping? I don't wanna carry the shopping on my bike dad.

Chris No, honestly, what about our holidays?

Sarah Yeah, that's a good point.

Chris Are we gonna take the train or we're going to fly or ...

Sarah How do we get to the airport with all those suitcases?

Chris Are you going to pay for all those tickets, yeah? Exactly.

Dad Why do you need a car to do that?

Chris Because Sarah has like so much luggage with her all the time ...

Sarah I do not.

Chris Yes, you do.

Dad To take it on holiday?

Sarah No. You just making it up.

→

Dad	Oh come on, just be realistic, think about it. I know you, you're, you're ... You're born in a different generation. You do really expect to have a car, a computer and all this other stuff and I think a lot of it is not necessary or at least we could share things instead of everybody owning ... their own car, their own computer..
Chris	I don't know about that ... I really don't know. But I did actually hear ... well, I did actually hear about something similar. But it doesn't require you to actually sell your own car. It's called something like, erm, rent your neighbour's car or using your neighbour's car or something like that. Let me just discuss this with you guys.
Sarah	OK.
Chris	This is the idea: You register online and, erm, basically you can just rent out your car to people who need it and they pay you know by the hour or however you want them to pay and you set your own rates and you only ever have to pay, you know, pay the organization mmh, whenever somebody uses the platform online to rent your car. But it doesn't require you to sell the car. So ...
Sarah	So you've got the freedom of having your car.
Chris	Yeah, exactly. Because I mean honestly as I said: as a family you do actually eventually need a car and if you don't have one and, you know, a situation occurs where you do need one desparately ...
Dad	Well, have you got any more details about it?
Chris	I dont know, I don't know where I read it, I dont' know what it costs but I do actually, I read about it, it's for free, its online registration's for free.
Dad	Can you find the details?
Chris	Yeah, I can just check online and you just pay for it whenever somebody rents your car.
Sarah	I think that sounds like a really good idea. Yeah, I think it's better than the whole car sharing scheme ...
Dad	Allright. Then shall we do that?
Sarah	Yeah, let's look into it.
Dad	OK, what about some breakfast?
Sarah	Yes, cornflakes, please.
Chris	Good idea.
Dad	Thank God for that.

a)

1	Dad	a) tells his kids that he is going to sell the family car.	
		b) wants to make a difference and help the environment.	✔
		c) wants to get fit.	
		d) wants to go by bike.	

2	Sarah	a) sees a problem with the shopping.	✔
		b) is 17 years old.	
		c) wants to take a taxi to get home after a party.	
		d) wants to go on holiday by car.	

3	Sarah	a) doesn't like Chris's idea.	
		b) wants to have driving lessons with her father.	✔
		c) wants her father to give her a car as a birthday present.	
		d) worries that she cannot take all her suitcases with her when they go on holiday.	

4	Chris	a) likes his father's idea.	
		b) would like to use public transport.	
		c) wants to go on holidays by plane.	
		d) only has some information about another car sharing system.	✔

b)

Dad: 2, 4, 5, 9

Chris: 1, 3, 4, 6, 7, 8, 10

Lerntipp **Listening Skills üben**

- Höre dir englische Songs an und versuche, einzelne Wörter oder auch Sätze zu verstehen.
- Höre sie immer wieder an und erschließe dir so immer mehr Text.
- Wenn du das Gefühl hast, dass ein spezielles Wort, das du nicht verstehst, sehr wichtig ist, kannst du auch im Wörterbuch nachschlagen.

LANGUAGE

1 WORDS The environment

a)

Mögliche Lösungen:

carbon dioxide, carbon footprint, global warming, emission, insulation, greenhouse

b)

Mögliche Lösungen:

Many people try to reduce their carbon footprint.

Global warming is one of the problems we have to deal with.

Good insulation is important for all houses.

2 GRAMMAR REVISION + An old woman is talking about cars

I can remember the times when nobody in our village had a car. And I still remember the day when the first car drove down the main street in our village. That was around the year 1938. Everybody ran into the street when the car came nearer. It was an attraction for everybody. Our family didn't have a car until 1955. My sister and I were very proud when our father arrived in front of our house with the new family car.

Today it's different. Almost every family has a car, some even have two. But things change: there are people who don't want a car. They use public transport because it is cheaper and it helps the environment.

I sold my car ten years ago when I was 80. And I gave my driving licence to the town hall on the same day.

Today I take a taxi when I need to go somewhere.

3 GRAMMAR REVISION + A project for parents and young people

There was an interesting project at Seaview High School last weekend. The day was announced on the internet as a hands-on day for children and their parents.

The police wanted to inform the families about the dangers of the internet and how they can protect themselves.

A policeman talked about safety on the internet and gave many examples of what can be done. Parents and children were asked to tell the others about their experience with the internet.

A second very important topic was social networking sites because they are used by more and more teenagers. Children were asked what they do first when they come home after school. They answered that they communicated on social networking sites for more than half an hour.

"The internet gives you a lot of freedom but it also takes people's time," the policeman said.

During the workshop the parents had to do several tasks. Many of them were helped by their children.

At the end, everybody was invited to ask questions, and the policeman answered them patiently.

MEDIATION

1 An energy day

Mögliche Lösung:

Tim Was steht da eigentlich über die EUSEW?

Du Das ist eine Initiative der Europäischen Kommission in Brüssel. Sie besteht seit 2006. (3P)

Tim Können wir das auch hier bei uns in Sachsen machen oder geht das nur in Brüssel?

Du Das geht auch bei uns. (1P)

Tim Ist das nun eine Woche oder ein Tag, den wir organisieren sollen?

Du Es ist ein Tag. (1P)

Tim Und es muss genau in der Zeit vom 18.–22. Juni sein? Da haben wir doch unsere Parisfahrt.

Du Es ist auch an den Wochenenden davor und danach möglich. (1P)

Tim Also gut, ich stell mir vor, wir könnten da was mit unserem Fußballverein machen und uns nebenbei etwas für die Vereinskasse verdienen. Was meinst du?

Du Das geht leider nicht, es darf kein Verdienst gemacht werden. (1P)

Tim Was für einen Nutzen hätten wir dann für unseren Verein überhaupt?

Du Die Leute werden auf uns aufmerksam, vielleicht bekommen wir neue Mitglieder und es wird wahrscheinlich auch ein Zeitungsartikel erscheinen. (3P)

Tim Das ist natürlich auch gut. Und was müssen wir tun, wenn wir mitmachen wollen?

Du Wir müssen uns anmelden und dann können wir ihnen unsere Projektidee mitteilen, die wir an dem Tag realisieren wollen. (2P)

2 Get on your bike

Mögliche Lösung:

The government wants to double the number of bikes in cities and towns within the next ten years. (2P) The project is called "RadKultur". (1P) They want more people to use their bikes and to make the bike more popular. (2P) A team of experts is going to make suggestions where to build more bike paths. (1P) The project will be realized in Tübingen, Lörrach and Mannheim first. (1P) They are thinking of competitions for good ideas and they want to have special activities at schools to make the bike more popular. (3P) Later they also want to have companies as their partner because they say that companies must learn to accept the bike too. (2P)

Lerntipp **Einen deutschen Text sinngemäß ins Englische übertragen**

Wenn du einen deutschen Text ins Englische übertragen sollst, musst du versuchen, dich von dem genauen Wortlaut der Sätze zu lösen. Deine Aufgabe besteht darin, den Sinn möglichst fehlerfrei auf Englisch wiederzugeben.
Weißt du ein bestimmtes Wort nicht, überlege, wie du den Satz anders ausdrücken kannst, ohne dass sich der Sinn ändert. Manchmal hilft es auch, den Satz ein wenig umzustellen.
Wenn du mit solchen Aufgaben noch Schwierigkeiten hast, kannst du immer wieder üben, kleine Äußerungen oder Sätze (z.B. aus der Zeitung) ins Englische zu übertragen. Benutze das Wörterbuch nur, wenn du gar nicht mehr weiter kommst.

WRITING

A car of your own?

Mögliche Lösung:

I have many friends who are thinking about having their own car. I am going to write about whether or not I would like to have a car of my own. (2P)

First, a car is very expensive. You have to buy petrol. You also have to pay a mechanic when your car is broken and you need somebody to repair it, for example. (3P)

Second, thinking of my carbon footprint, I do not think it is good to have a car because I will probably use my car alone very often. This is not good for the environment, and I think everybody should do something about pollution. (4P)

On the other hand, you can do car sharing with your friends. It is also comfortable to have a car because it is always in front of your house and you can also transport things easily. Going by car can save a lot of time. However, using public transport is sometimes even quicker than a car. (5P)

To sum up, I think that it is better for the environment to use public transport if you have the chance. I do not want to spend so much money on a car either. So this means I don't want a car of my own. (3P)

SPEAKING

09 How ecology-minded are we?

First let me describe the cartoon:

The cartoon shows a scene in a school. A girl and her teacher are standing in a classroom in front of the board. The teacher is an older woman who is looking surprised. She has some paper and a pen in her hands. The girl is smaller than the teacher and she is looking up to her. She has an open book in her hands and she is asking her teacher a question: "Explain to me again why our ecology textbook is printed on dead trees." The teacher looks as if she doesn't know the answer.

Second I'd like to say what the cartoon is about and what the message could be.

The cartoon is about saving the environment and stopping global warming. The girl is talking about her ecology book. The ecology book deals with environmental problems and I think in the ecology book you can find many suggestions what we can do to save the environment. And I can imagine that one of the tips is to save trees because trees use CO_2 and produce clean air.

Now the girl wants to know from the teacher why her ecology book is printed on 'dead trees' as trees were needed to produce the paper for the book, yet the message in the book is to save trees.
The girl might represent the younger generation who may be able to teach the older generation to think differently about how they can help to save the environment (e.g. no paper in classrooms, using computers rather than books etc.)

Now I'd like to talk about my opinion:

I like the cartoon because it makes clear that very often it's easy to give tips about how to save the environment but it's difficult to carry out this advice in real life.
I think we all need books but on the other hand we should try to save paper. I think we can save paper if we think before printing things from the computer.

Now you

Mögliche Lösung:

Let me describe the cartoon first:

The cartoon shows a scene in a shoe shop. A man is sitting there and trying on shoes. The shop assistant is sitting on the floor and showing him different shoes. He has one shoe in his hand and explains to the customer: "We have a new line of environmentally-friendly shoes. They leave a low carbon footprint." The customer is older than the shop assistant. He's wearing a tie and looks like a business man. He looks as if he doesn't understand the shop assistant's message. (7P)

Second I'd like to say what the cartoon is about and what the message could be:

The cartoon is about keeping our carbon footprint low. I think it wants to show that sometimes things are sold with a special message. In this case, the message wants to make the man think that he is doing something for the environment when he buys the shoes. The message could also be that you can keep your carbon footprint low when you buy something special which may be a bit more expensive. In fact your carbon footprint is still high, of course, but with the new thing you can feel better if you think of your carbon footprint. (6P)

In my opinion, this cartoon is really good. Of course, everybody knows that you can't keep your carbon footprint low with a pair of shoes. This message makes me laugh. But everybody should pay attention when he or she buys something. The message is not to believe that you can buy something and the result is that your carbon footprint is low. No, you must become active yourself. (5P)

My family and I try to save energy whenever we can. When leaving a room, we always turn off the lights. And we leave the car in the garage whenever it makes sense. (2P)

Lösungen A

LISTENING

10 Great success for students

Reporter Hello everybody out there. This is Ben on "Radio for friends". I'm here at *Midland School* today. Maybe you've heard about the huge problems students have been having recently with public transport. For those of you who don't know: every March and October the city's bus timetables are changed. So far the changes have been small and haven't really affected the students.
But this year was very different. The changes meant that students from the northern areas of the city had to wait nearly an hour for their bus home. As we heard on the nine o'clock news, the bus company has since decided to change the [time] tables again following huge protests from [sic; besser wäre *by*] students, teachers and parents from the school. So, let's find out just how they stood up for their rights!
I have Steve with me here. Hi, Steve, tell me how the timetable changes affected you.

Steve Oh, yeah, well, I live in the north, about 7 miles away from school. I used to catch bus number 13 at 4.05 after school. And I'd get home around 4.40 every day. But with the new timetable, you know, I had to wait until 4.50 and got home at 5.27. The worst thing was that the school closes at 4 and I always had to wait outside. Nobody else had to wait as long as I did and I couldn't do anything the whole time, not even homework or anything. Well, I could listen to music, but that was it. And when I got home, it was already dinner time and then I had to do my homework afterwards. So, like, there was no time for hanging out with friends or playing football or anything. It was really bad, so I'm pretty pleased that they've changed the timetable.

Reporter Oh, yes, I can believe you. It must have been terrible. So, now Melissa, hi! What's been your experience?

Melissa Hi. Yeah, umm, I also live in the north and I usually catch bus number 28 to go to school. When the timetable changed, I had to get up 45 minutes earlier. And I had to walk to a different bus stop which was so far away. And I got home 35 minutes later in the evening. That adds up to a lot of time every day! It was bad for getting my homework done and because I never had time to play tennis anymore. And the worst thing was that I had to wait in school for ages every morning before lessons began. It was a complete waste of time! I pay a lot of money for my bus ticket and I think I have the right to get to school at an acceptable time. I couldn't believe that the bus company changed the timetable just to save money or something like that. So, yeah, so then a few of us decided to do something about the situation.

Reporter Yes, and you've been successful. We'll be hearing about that in a minute when I talk to one of your teachers, Mr Burton. I can really understand that you're angry, though.
Thanks, Melissa. Speak to you later.

a)

Mögliche Lösungen:

1 Name the months when timetables change.	March and October
2 Give information about the experience with the timetable changes so far. *(2 facts)*	small and haven't really affected the students
3 Say when the listeners found out that the bus company had reacted to the protests?	in the news at nine
4 Give reasons why the bus company reacted.	protest of students, letter to newspapers, students talked to the manager
5 Give two facts about where Steve lives.	in the north, 7 miles away from school
6 Name three reasons why the new timetable was bad for Steve.	1 had to wait until 4.50 2 had to wait outside school 3 couldn't meet his friends anymore
7 Name three ways the new timetable affected Melissa.	1 had to get up 45 minutes earlier 2 had to walk further to the bus stop 3 got home 35 minutes later
8 Explain why Melissa thought that the bus company's timetable changes were not OK.	she pays a lot of money for her ticket

11 ***Reporter*** Welcome back. With me is Mr Burton, a teacher at the school. Mr Burton, what did you do with your students in class to react against the changes to the bus timetables?

Mr Burton Hello, yes, umm … it's very important for our school to teach the students the ideas behind democracy. We try to run the school democratically too and we allow our students to have their say by encouraging them to talk about any issues or problems in class. These discussions often become quite lively debates. With the bus timetable situation, it was very interesting to see that it wasn't just one or two students who complained about the changes but almost the whole class had something to say. We tried to think about what we could do and talked about how we might be able to change the bus company's decision. And after a long discussion we agreed on different things:

The first was that the students wanted to write a letter to local newspapers and inform them about the situation. Then they planned to go and talk to the manager of the bus service. And finally they decided to go into town and tell people on the streets about it all, so they created colourful posters.

Reporter OK, all those sound like good plans. And how did they get on?

Mr Burton Well, there was a huge response to their activities: a lot of people answered their letter in the newspaper. And nearly all of them agreed that the timetable changes were unfair. The manager really listened to what the students had to say. I think he was quite impressed by their attitude. And on that single Saturday morning in town, they managed to collect 388 signatures against the change to the timetables.

I think that the activities were a positive thing because they made the students realize how important it is to have their say. At the time, they didn't know if they'd be successful or not. But they were, and the bus times have been changed back again. I feel that the whole situation was very important for them to experience how getting involved and fighting for your rights can lead to success. Even if it does mean hard work. And for myself, I have to say: I'm so proud of them, they did a really good job!

Reporter Oh yes, I'd agree with that. Thank you Mr Burton. It was great to hear such a fantastic success story!

Now we have a mother on the phone. Hi Mrs Miller. So, what did you like about this protest?

→

Mrs Miller Hi. Yes, well, I very much liked the way the whole process worked. I was surprised at how quickly the students reacted. I think it's brilliant that the school and the teachers give them room to discuss things like that in class. The teachers were so ready to help the students, which was great. But what really impressed me was that even though the bus timetable changes hadn't affected all the students negatively, many students still stood up and had their say. They supported their classmates. I think that showed that the school is doing a great job of teaching the kids how democracy works.

I also liked the way they tried to put the public in the picture. The students talked to people in their free time, you know, they tried to get them to support their protest and they asked for signatures. And, luckily, they were really polite and everything went off very peacefully. There was no vandalism or anything like that. I think it all went very well. And I'm happy that the bus times have been changed again!

Reporter Yeah, you have a child who was very much affected by the changes, don't you?

Mrs Miller Haha, yes I do.

Reporter Well, it looks like the students' hard work has paid off! What a great result. Thanks for coming on the show, Mrs Miller, and I hope Melissa enjoys getting up a bit later again! So, next we're going to play you some music ...

b)

Mögliche Lösungen:

1 teachers encourage their students to talk about their problems

2 wrote an open letter to the newspaper, went and talked to the manager of the bus company, informed people in the streets, created posters

3 people answered the open letter, the manager of the bus company listened to the students, the students got 388 signatures

4 the students could see that it is important to have your say

5 how quickly the students reacted, teachers were ready to help, students supported their classmates, no vandalism

LANGUAGE

1 WORDS The wrong word

1 political party
2 to make sth up
3 trade
4 to make sense
5 narrator
6 democracy

2 WORDS Creating new words

1 sense	sensible, sensitive
2 poor	poverty
3 (to) think	a thought
4 (to) annoy	annoying
5 (to) debate	a debate
6 (to) apologize	apology
7 (to) own	owner
8 (to) speak	a speech
9 (to) feel	feeling
10 discrimination	(to) discriminate

3 GRAMMAR REVISION + A discussion about bus times

Before the campaign

1 I will have to catch the early bus at 7.10 if I want to be at school on time.
2 If the bus company doesn't change the times, we will go on strike.
3 I won't be able to take part in the dancing lessons any more if I don't get home until 5.20 pm.

During the campaign

1 If we talked to the bus company, perhaps they would change the times again.
2 We could tell a lot of people in town if we went to the market square on Saturday morning.
3 If we collected a lot of signatures from people in town, we could give them to the bus company.

After the campaign

1 If the students hadn't done anything about the new bus times, some of them wouldn't have had time for hobbies after school.
2 If the students hadn't written the letter to the newspaper, the public wouldn't have known about the issue.
3 If the students hadn't done such a good job, the bus company wouldn't have reacted.

Lerntipp **if-Sätze**

- Sieh dir die drei Sätze vom Handhinweis vor der Aufgabe nochmals an und schreibe sie in dein Lernheft.
- Schreibe unter jede Verbform den Namen der Zeit. So erkennst du, wie die Zeiten in den drei Arten von if-Sätzen verwendet werden.
- Bist du noch unsicher, dann sieh im Grammar File 9 auf S. 171 in deinem Englischbuch nach.

4 GRAMMAR Teens speak out

"Teens Speak Out" began last Saturday morning with a short speech and an explanation of Rule No. 1: "You adults out there aren't allowed to speak now," presenter Phil Cross told the audience.

During the discussion, students shared their opinions about many different topics. They spoke about communication with teachers and the head teacher, the importance of sports and about school safety.

14-year-old student Alan said that it was necessary to improve contact with the head teacher. "The only time you hear from the head teacher is during an assembly, or when she's addressing all the students, or when there's something going on that she doesn't like," he said.

Sue, aged 15, agreed. She wanted the head teacher to see and recognize the good work that is done by many students. "It's time the head teacher changed something. At the moment she only speaks to us when something is going wrong. Things would be much better if she saw the good work and talked to the students about their success."

5 GRAMMAR REVISION + Word order

1 Last week we had a great meeting. / We had a great meeting last week.
2 First of all, we took a picture for the School Yearbook.
3 Then there was a long discussion about the school shop.
4 Nearly all the students enjoy buying things at the shop.
5 We heard what they like and what needs to be improved.
6 After that we talked about the youth club. / We talked about the youth club after that.
7 Unfortunately, we didn't have time to finish the discussion.
8 So we are going to meet again next Saturday.

6 Everyday English: Solving conflicts

Mögliche Lösungen:

You ▶ start the conversation	*Excuse me, Anna, can I have a word with you?*
You ▶ name the problem	As you can see, I'd like to cook my dinner but I can't because the kitchen is in an awful mess. I think you used the kitchen just before me. (2P)
Anna ▶ disagree that there is a problem and start talking about how wonderful your dinner was	Yes, that's right. But where's the problem? It isn't in such a mess. I also had to clean up the kitchen because the last person had not done it. And I had such wonderful spaghetti, it was great! Oh I love spaghetti. Do you like spaghetti with tomato sauce too? (4P)
You ▶ explain the problem again	Yes, I do. But the problem is that you left the kitchen so dirty that I can't cook. I don't want to clean up your mess. That's the problem. (3P)
Anna ▶ apologize, find a way to solve the problem	I'm sorry. I should have cleaned the kitchen. I'll do it right away. Is that OK? (3P)
You ▶ end the conflict and make a suggestion	It's OK for me. And I'll help you. And maybe we can agree to clean the kitchen after we use it? (3P)
Anna ▶ say thank you and say that you like the idea	OK, that's a good idea and very nice of you, thank you. (2P)

WRITING

1 Young people and their attitude towards the internet

Mögliche Lösung:

The internet has become very popular in the last few years, especially with young people. (1P)

However, there are teenagers who see the internet critically. Some say it is not safe because their personal information might be misused. Another argument is that surfing the internet costs too much and also takes too much time which could be used for other things, e.g. volunteering to help others. (4P)

I surf the internet almost every day. I communicate with my friends on social networking sites and I use it for collecting information. (3P)

I do not agree with most of the critical statements. Communicating with your friends is important and can be very quick on the internet. And, for example, if you need information for a presentation, surfing the internet is a lot quicker than going to the library. We have a flat rate, so it is not expensive. (4P)

Of course, everybody should be careful with the personal information they put on the internet. This can be very dangerous. (1P)

To sum up, I would say that young people need the internet to lead a modern life. The internet is great for communication and for information. (2P)

Lerntipp **So kannst du beim Writing besser werden:**

- Ein ganz wichtiger Schritt, um beim **Writing** besser zu werden, ist die Überprüfung deines Textes. So kannst du feststellen, an welchen Stellen du deinen Text nochmal überarbeiten kannst und worauf du beim nächsten Mal besonders achten solltest.

Überprüfe wichtige Punkte anhand der folgenden Liste.

- Du kannst diese Liste immer wieder verwenden.
- Unten hast du Gelegenheit, eigene Punkte einzufügen, auf die du in Zukunft besonders achten willst.

• Brief / E-Mail: Anrede, Grußformel? • Bericht / Geschichte / Diskussion: Überschrift?		
• Aufgabenstellung genau beachtet?		
• Einleitung / einleitender Satz am Anfang?		
• Text durch Absätze logisch strukturiert?		
• Unterschiedliche Satzstrukturen (z.B. Relativsätze, Sätze mit **linking words**) verwendet?		
• Rechtschreibung und Grammatik (Zeiten, Wortstellung) okay?		
• Sinnvolle Länge der Sätze?		
• Brief / E-Mail: Schlussformel? • Bericht / Geschichte / Diskussion: Schlusssatz?		
•		
•		
•		

2 What about an environmental group at your school?

Mögliche Lösung:

Hello Steve,

Thanks a lot for your email. Yes, I like your idea. I think it's a really good thing if students get involved at their schools. (1P) It's a great way to do things together and learn how to speak out. I also think that doing something for the environment should be a normal thing for everybody. (3P)

I can imagine starting such a group at our school. I need to ask the head teacher of course. But that's no problem. (3P) There are many things we could do. We could collect used paper, we could collect plastic things and we could inform other students about important issues, for example how to save energy in the classroom. (The head teacher will like this!) (3P)

What activities does your group do? (1P) Write soon.

Bye, ...

READING

Report on young Londoners

a)

Mögliche Lösungen:

1 What were four of the topics of the survey?	education, safety, transport, getting involved
2 Who was interviewed *(2 facts)*?	more than 1000 Londoners aged 11–16
3 Why did they need the 2004 survey?	to compare the 2009 results with 2004.

b)

1 When talking about living in London, shopping	a) is the most important thing for young Londoners.	
	b) only comes second.	✔
	c) is not mentioned.	
2 The 2009 survey shows that	a) most young Londoners have tried to change something in their area.	✔
	b) it's necessary to activate more young people.	
	c) many young people think you can't change anything by getting involved.	
3 If you compare the results of 2004 and 2009,	a) in 2004, fewer young people said that they could take part in decisions at schools.	✔
	b) more people felt safe in 2004.	
	c) issues about the environment were not a problem in 2009.	
4 When talking about safety and crime,	a) many young people say that they have been victim to violent crime.	
	b) teenagers hanging around is one of the biggest problems.	
	c) many young Londoners would like the police to be more present in London.	✔
5 The survey says that	a) most young people walk to school although they could use the bus for free.	
	b) young Londoners don't walk because of the Zip Card.	
	c) the bus is the favourite form of transport.	✔
6 When talking about the environment,	a) young Londoners make it clear that parks are very important.	✔
	b) waste and air quality are the most important issues.	
	c) more young people mentioned the pollution of the waterways as a problem than rubbish.	
7 Many young people think	a) that the quality of their schools could be better.	
	b) that they will find a job in the London area.	
	c) that London cannot provide good opportunities in difficult times.	✔

LANGUAGE

1 WORDS Have your say – a discussion

The public can take part in another discussion on an important topic on Wednesday, 7 July at 7.30 pm. This time the discussion will be on the mosquito device which has been installed in front of the youth club. As usual, interesting guests will take part and discuss the topic, for example Mr Pit Hank, a politician here in our town. Mr Hank thinks the mosquito device is a useful thing and that it makes sense where it is. Then there are Tom and Nicholas, two students who have started a petition against the mosquito device. And there is Mrs Felder. Although Mrs Felder lives near the youth club, she supports the campaign against the mosquito device. Also there will be Mr Jeff Saltman who says that the mosquito device can't be removed unless the young people get a new place to meet. Peter Smith, the well-known presenter from Radio Young, will lead the discussion.

Place: Grattan's Hotel 24, Swansea Road.

2 WORDS Students talking in a school break

1 I think Jo is very good at presenting topics.
2 I'm afraid of failing our Maths test tomorrow.
3 Mrs Sutter is a really good teacher. Her attitude towards the students is excellent.
4 I can't blame anybody else for my bad mark in English – I have just been too lazy the last few months.
5 I'm glad that Sue apologized to me for her bad behaviour.
6 I read in the school magazine that the number of hours spent on homework at our school has risen by ten per cent in the last two years.
7 I don't think that Mr Gardener is prejudiced against any of the students, he's very fair.
8 John is really interested in German history, he knows so much!
9 Mark will throw a big party on Friday evening.
10 Did you know that Mrs Sutter is married to a Swiss man?

3 GRAMMAR REVISION + Talking about a school shop

Mary	Monica
The shop will help students to work together.	The shop won't work because students buy their school things in the supermarket.
If you have forgotten an exercise book, you will be able to buy it at school.	The students won't spend their free time working in the shop. They will only work there during school hours.
The students will do something useful in their free time.	The students won't be able to sell things cheaply enough.

4 GRAMMAR REVISION + Talking about the future

a)

1 Look, here is the ticket for my flight. I'm flying to Spain tomorrow.

2 Lisa has just given me a call. I think she'll be late for dinner.

3 I'm sorry, mum. I haven't had time to tidy up my room. I'll do it after school. I promise!

4 Nick's just told me about his problems at school. We're going to talk to the teachers in a few days.

5 It's terribly cold, isn't it? But it'll be warmer next week.

6 It's Sue's birthday in a few days. I'm going to send her a nice birthday card.

7 We've already booked our holidays for next year. We're going to Florida again.

8 This year Susanna was chosen to play the main part in the school theatre production. I'm sure that next year it'll be you, Alice.

b)

Mögliche Lösungen:

1 I'm going to talk to my teacher tomorrow.

2 I think John will be our coach next year.

3 I'm meeting friends this evening.

5 GRAMMAR REVISION + About Ann's presentation

a)

1 I think she was a bit nervous.

2 She had prepared her presentation well.

3 Ann talked in a way that I could follow her presentation easily.

4 Personally, I liked the way she kept looking at the audience.

5 The outline was worked out carefully.

6 The photos she showed were fantastic.

b)

Mögliche Lösungen:

1 The presentation was great/interesting/bad/boring. (adjective)

2 She talked too quietly/loudly/slowly/quickly/fast. (adverb)

3 I think people liked listening because the topic was so interesting/exciting. (adjective)

MEDIATION

Have your say on Highway 2A

Mögliche Lösungen:

1 Die Verkehrsbehörde erstellt derzeit einen Bericht über die Sicherheit auf dem Highway 2A. Die Gemeinde soll auch ihre Meinung abgeben und wurde zum Workshop eingeladen. (3P)

2 Sie werden über die Gefahren des Highway 2A befragt. (1P)

3 Das Treffen findet in Form eines Workshops statt. (1P)

4 Die Bürger müssen sich registrieren. (1P)

5 Die Bürger können sich auch online oder via E-Mail beteiligen. (2P)

6 Es wurden Mitteilungen an die Haushalte verteilt, die auf den Workshop hingewiesen haben. Sie enthielten auch die Telefonnummer, unter der man sich registrieren kann. (3P)

SPEAKING

12 At the end of school

Hi, my name's Paul, and I'm talking about my experiences at Mittelberg Schule today. I've been at this school for six years now. I'm going to divide my talk into 4 parts. First, I'm going to talk about the first couple of years. Then I'm going to talk about years 7 and 8, then about years 9 and 10. I'll end my talk with a little summary.

When I first started at this school, I was 10 years old. I was really worried about the school, new teachers, new classmates and of course about the new subjects. I didn't know what it was going to be like. But very soon I found a good friend who I did everything with. And our teachers were really helpful trying to settle us into the new situation. They didn't just try to help us with our learning, but lots of them also listened to our problems and tried to find ways to solve them. So after a few months everything was OK. My worries were gone and I felt OK at the new school.

Now, years 7 and 8. Those were pretty hard years, I have to say. To be honest, school definitely wasn't my favourite thing at that time. I didn't work enough at home or at school, so my marks got bad and I got lazier and lazier. You probably know the situation, right? It's very difficult to get out of it. So I didn't want to go to school any more. But my parents kept telling me it was the right thing to stay and I would miss so many opportunities if I left. So in the end, I stayed.

This leads me to years 9 and 10 now. They were better. My teachers encouraged me to start thinking about what I wanted to do after school – like which job would be good for me, what I wanted to do with my life and all that. I realized that I had to work harder at school if I wanted to get a job I'm interested in. So, I needed good marks at the end of year 10. That thought made me work harder, really hard sometimes. And it worked! My marks got better and now I have a good report, and I hope it will be enough to become a computer engineer.

To sum up my talk about my years at school, I have to say I've had quite a good time here. I could have done with more help in years 7 and 8 because they were really hard. But I somehow got through them, I just kept going and tried my best. Maybe some careers advice would have been good, it might have helped me to see what I wanted to do later on. But, anyway, I could make without it! I think Mittelberg Schule is a good school with good teachers. And I'd be really happy if my talk helps you to think positively if you ever have a few problems at some point at school. Remember: never give up!

Thank you very much.

Now you

Mögliche Lösung:

Hello, my name is Laura and I would like to talk about the last six years at this school. I'm going to divide my talk into four parts. First, I'm going to talk about my first two years here. Then I would like to say something about years 7 and 8, then about 9 and 10. To finish my talk, I will give you a short summary. (2P)

When I first came here, I was very nervous and very sad. On the one hand, I was happy because my best friend Rebecca also came to this school. On the other hand, I missed my other friends. I could only meet them after school. (2P) I have to say that I had problems here at first. My marks were not very good, and I had problems following the lessons. (1P) Some other students in my class were very good and often they had already done what was new for me when I came here. (1P) But Rebecca and I started to learn together, that was very good. (1P) Our teachers were also friendly – and some of them were very strict! But after a while it became easier for me. (1P)

Now I come to years 7 and 8. They were fun! We went on a class trip, and I got to know many people from my class much better. That also made our lessons easier, and school suddenly became a place I wanted to go to. (2P) Well, I have to say that it was more because of the other students, not really because of the lessons! But the lessons were also OK and the teachers were always there to help us. (2P) Rebecca and I still had our learning group and others joined us, so we had a lot of fun working together. But our marks – yes, well, they didn't get better. But anyway, those years were great! (1P)

Now let me talk about years 9 and 10. They were much harder. My parents wanted me to get good marks at school because they wanted me to have a good job. (2P) This was difficult. My marks were always OK, not very good but OK, I was happy with them, and friends were more important to me anyway. (1P) But then I had to learn very hard, and my parents always wanted to see my homework and all that. This wasn't really fun anymore. But, yes, I have to say that they were right when they wanted me to become better. My marks became really good, and now I'm going to do an apprenticeship as a mechanic. I hope I will like it! (2P)

To sum up my talk, I have to say that it was really fun being here. The teachers are helpful, and the students are very cool! You can have so much fun here! You also have many chances at this school and you can ask the teachers to help you. (2P)

I hope I was able to give you a good idea about my school life. Thank you very much. (1P)